D1562395

OUR CONNECTION WITH THE SAINTS

"To whom of those great, and powerful and glorious do so many people come every day, as they come to the blind eldress Matrona, who laid in bed all her life? There is not one world ruler who receives such a daily pilgrimage of thousands of people; no one stands all night to touch their tombs." There is no real connection with worldly heroes, the Patriarch continued, "but a real connection is preserved with the Saints; the Saints are present in our lives."

— *His Holiness Patriarch Kirill*
of Moscow and All Russia

August 25, 2021

To: Ariane Trifunovic Montemuro

Dear Ariane,

I was absolutely thrilled to discover your new book on Saint Matrona the Blind. She has been one of my favorite Saints for many years. I have always been frustrated not being able to find a book about her written in English. Then I found your book!

I loved the book so much. I feel your sincere love for Saint Matrona in every page, and I can certainly relate! In fact, I even read your book twice! Plus, now I often pray the Matrona Akathist you provide readers of your book. All of this combined — I feel, has drawn me even closer to the Saint.

Recently, I was reflecting on her holy and incredibly inspirational life. Then, I pictured the extreme juxtaposition of this current God-less state of education that exists in today's world. This thought literally made me sick. Right at that moment, I decided to make a promise to our beloved Saint Matrona.

I told her that if she could please ask the Lord to help me get my Doctorate in Education degree then I would eventually devise and execute a plan to open an international school named after her.

Guess what! I got accepted today to a Ph.D. program in Education! I had to share my joy. Once again, I thank you, Ariane, for writing this book. My continued friendship with Saint Matrona is a blessing.

I believe this Saint will inspire others around the world! More than anything, I hope your book helps more people learn about this great Saint of God.

With love in Christ,

JULIE ANN MIRSE
Dean of Instruction
Future Doctor of Education in Leadership

*Ariane Trifunovic Montemuro's books on Orthodox Christian
Saints are being sold as fundraisers for
Holy Trinity Seminary in Jordanville, New York.*

*Ariane is pictured here with Bishop Luke and
Father Innocent holding* Debt of Love,
her book on Tsar-Martyr Nicholas II and family.

THE AUTHOR'S INVITATION...

This book you are holding about Saint Matrona the Blind is the first of its kind in the English language.

Although blind from birth, Holy Eldress Matrona possessed a multitude of spiritual gifts through the grace of God. This Russian Saint not only foresaw the future but also clearly saw the souls of the people who sought her out for help in their lives. **We need Saint Matrona *now* more than ever**. She teaches us how to acquire true spiritual vision in our lives. It is this spiritual vision that will save us during these God-less times in which we currently live.

I invite you — through the pages of this book — to come to know, love, and call upon Saint Matrona for help in your life. At the end of this book, an Akathist prayer is provided to help you do so. She has promised to respond to every sincere, heartfelt call because *she is our true friend in Christ*.

Matrona cares about the salvation of each of our souls. She will help us with any situation in our lives and will draw us back from false ways in order to keep us on the true path to Christ.

I feel her continued, loving presence and help in my life. I know you will too.

ARIANE TRIFUNOVIC MONTEMURO
Nashville, Tennessee 2021

Father Tikhon holding an icon of Saint Matrona the Blind.

LETTER FROM FATHER TIKHON

The Holy Matrona of Moscow is lovingly known among the faithful as "Matushka-Matronushka." Her memory is celebrated on May 2nd. She was canonized quite recently, in 1998. Even before that date, her grave was frequently visited by the faithful who sought her help and support. Everyone knew that Saint Matrona helps those who seek her help with sincerity. She was blind from childhood, and as a result of this, she dedicated her life to prayer to God. The Lord gave her the great gift of performing miracles. She helped people during her lifetime, and she continues to do so now. She is petitioned for help in everyday life situations, when it seems that there is no hope. In America the veneration of Saint Matrona is also widespread. We see icons of Saint Matronushka in all the churches in the USA, with many of the faithful praying before these icons. I believe that Saint Matrona of Moscow will help you too.

FATHER TIKHON

Very Reverend Abbot Tikhon Gayfudinov is the Rector of The Hermitage of The Holy Protection, Buena Vista Township, New Jersey.

Saint Matrona of Moscow — commemorated May 2 —
is most properly depicted in Orthodox iconography with
eyes open, both representing the far-seeing eyes of her soul and
also her physical vision that will be restored in the resurrection.

Troparion of Saint Matrona of Moscow

Chosen by the Holy Spirit from your swaddling clothes, O blessed Eldress Matrona. / Thou didst receive bodily weakness and blindness from God for spiritual cleansing. / Thou wast enriched with the gift of foresight and wonderworking and hast been adorned with an incorruptible crown from the Lord. / Therefore we offer thee crowns of praise, in gratitude crying out: / "Rejoice O righteous mother Matrona, fervent intercessor before God for us!"

Ikos 1

An angel in the flesh was thou revealed to be, O blessed Matrona, fulfilling the will of God. Though thou wast born in a bodily blindness, yet the Lord who maketh wise the blind and loveth the righteous enlightened thy spiritual eyes that thou mightest serve His people and the things of God were made manifest through thee. Wherefore with love we sing to thee such things as these: Rejoice, chosen one of God from thy youth; Rejoice, thou who didst shine forth with the grace of the Holy Spirit from thy cradle. Rejoice, thou who wast enriched with the gift of miracles even as a child; Rejoice thou who wast filled with wisdom from God most high. Rejoice, thou who foresawest the will of God with noetic eyes; Rejoice, thou who didst put to shame the wise of this age who are blinded in mind. Rejoice, thou who ledest deluded souls back toward God; Rejoice, thou who assuagest sorrow and affliction. **Rejoice O righteous mother Matrona**, **fervent intercessor before God for us.**[i]

БЛАЖЕННАЯ СТАРИЦА МАТРОНА

*Saint Matrona the Blind, "The People's Saint,"
has the reputation of being a Saint who helps anyone
who asks with a sincere heart.*

SAINT MATRONA THE BLIND
Our Friend in Christ

ARIANE TRIFUNOVIC MONTEMURO

Ideas into Books: Westview
Kingston Springs, Tennessee

Printed with the blessing of

His Grace

Bishop L O N G I N

+ + +

Ideas into Books®
W E S T V I E W
P.O. Box 605
Kingston Springs, TN 37082
www.publishedbywestview.com

ISBN 978-1-62880-213-9

First edition, October 2021

Please note that original spellings have been maintained
from all source materials.

Cover Design by
Ariane Trifunovic Montemuro.

Graphic Design by
Elaine P. Millen, TeknoLink Marketing Services, Charlotte, N.C.

The authors thanks Elena Smirnova for permission to publish her icon of
Saint Matrona on the cover of this book.
https://www.etsy.com/shop/russianorthodoxicons

The author thanks Holy Trinity Seminary, Jordanville, N.Y.,
for permission to use the Akathist to Saint Matrona.

The author thanks her husband, Anthony Montemuro, M.D.,
for his editorial services.

Due to permissions and public domain issues,
the quotations in this book are from the King James Version
instead of from the Orthodox Study Bible.

FOREWORD BY
HIS GRACE, BISHOP LUKE

His Grace, Bishop Luke of Syracuse
Rector of Holy Trinity Seminary and
Abbot of Holy Trinity Monastery
Jordanville, New York

REGARDING BLESSED MATRONA OF MOSCOW

Blessed Matrona of Moscow is currently one of the most venerated contemporary Saints of Russia. Even beyond Russia's borders, her intercession is sought by countless Orthodox Christians.

Saint Matrona was born blind into a poor family before the Communist Revolution. Her life was difficult to begin with due to her handicap and her poverty. Nevertheless, from her youth she was dedicated to God and spent her life in prayer and fasting.

She came to know Saint John of Kronstadt, who recognized her saintly attributes and predicted her saintly life.

During the worst of the Communist persecution of the Church and its faithful, she remained steadfast and became a light for the Orthodox faithful. People turned to her for advice, and she fearlessly consoled them during the severe repressions of the Soviet government.

From her youth she had the gifts of prophecy, spiritual vision and healing. She helped countless people in her lifetime. From the age of 17 she could no longer walk, but she received thousands of people at her home.

Saint Matrona died in 1952. Her grave became a place of pilgrimage. Later, her relics were transferred to the Holy Protection Convent in Moscow, where countless crowds of people, forming daily long lines that go out into the streets, wait to venerate her relics.

In our turbulent days, which in some ways seem to be similar to the uproars in Russia, let us turn to Blessed Matrona, asking her intercession and prayers for us of the last times.

+LUKE, Bishop of Syracuse
Abbot of Holy Trinity Monastery
Rector of Holy Trinity Seminary
Jordanville, New York

**This book is a fundraiser for
Holy Trinity Seminary.**
Donations to Holy Trinity Seminary in
Jordanville, New York can be sent to:
Holy Trinity Seminary
P.O. Box 36
1407 Robinson Road
Jordanville, NY 13361

Holy Trinity Orthodox Seminary is an institution of higher learning under the jurisdiction of the Russian Orthodox Church Outside Russia. The mission of Holy Trinity Orthodox Seminary is to serve the Russian Orthodox Church Outside Russia by preparing students for service to the Church as clergy, monastics, choir directors, cantors, iconographers, and lay leaders. To learn more about Holy Trinity Orthodox Seminary, log onto their website: *www.hts.edu*.

A MESSAGE REGARDING DONATIONS

Once again, our dear friend Ariane has written another wonderful book — ***Saint Matrona the Blind: Our Friend in Christ*** — from her heart, with the simple goal of inspiring her readers to become better acquainted with, and to pray for the intercession of, one of the great modern-day Saints of the Church, Saint Matrona the Blind of Moscow.

In return for this labor of love, she asks nothing for herself, but rather encourages her readers to honor the memory and the good works of Saint Matrona by making a donation to the Seminary Scholarship Fund at Holy Trinity Orthodox Seminary in Jordanville, New York, specifically to directly assist our seminarians meet the costs of their education.

Realizing that our students cannot apply for any government loans to assist with their expenses while studying in seminary, Ariane has also supported this cause by donating many copies of her previous book *Debt of Love* to our retail bookstore, as well as all of the proceeds from the outside sales of this work to benefit the Tsar-Martyr Nicholas, II Scholarship Fund, which she herself created in 2018.

You can make a donation by mail to: Holy Trinity Orthodox Seminary, P.O. Box 36, Jordanville, NY 13361, or electronically made securely through our website at https://hts.edu/support or through PayPal or through our HTOS Facebook page. Please be sure to indicate "Student Financial Aid — Saint Matrona" in the comments with your donation.

On behalf of our rector, Bishop Luke, our dean, our faculty, and particularly our students, I would like to thank you in advance for your kindness and generosity.

Feel free to reach out to me with any questions you may have. We encourage you to visit our historic monastery, seminary, and museum, located on a sprawling 1,000-acre campus in picturesque upstate New York.

Love in Christ,
DEACON MICHAEL PAVUK
Director of Development
mpavuk@hts.edu
570-466-0009

The author pictured here with Father Deacon Michael Pavuk,
Director of Development, Holy Trinity Seminary,
Jordanville, New York.

CONTENTS

DEDICATION

This book is dedicated to the
greatest of all the Saints,
the Most Holy Mother of God.

The wonderworking icon of the Theotokos,
the "Searcher for the Lost", written in 1915
at the direction of Saint Matrona of Moscow.
(https://www.pokrov-monastir.ru)

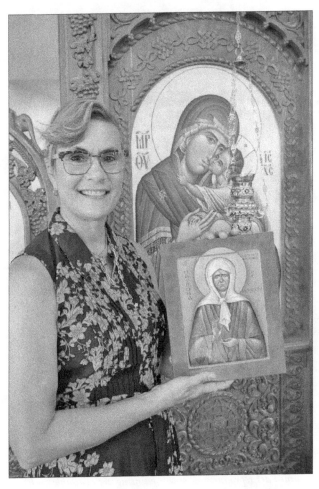

The author is pictured here in
Saint Petka Serbian Orthodox Church Nashville, Tennessee
holding her family icon of Saint Matrona the Blind.

(This icon of Saint Matrona was painted by
the hand of iconographer, Janet Jaime, eleousa@cox.net)

ST. MATRONA THE BLIND

This oil painting of Saint Matrona is by the author,
Ariane Trifunovic Montemuro. It currently resides with the
Jevtović family of Chicago, Illinois.
Framed art reproductions of this painting are available on Ebay
at https://ebay.to/3EA2VYT.

INTRODUCTION:
MATRONUSHKA
OUR FRIEND IN CHRIST

INTRODUCTION:
GOD GAVE US HIS SAINTS AS WEAPONS IN OUR LIVES

Our Friends in Christ, Intercede for us!

Today's world is troubling. We are constantly bombarded by attacks from the evil one. However, we should never lose hope. Instead, we should look to befriend a Holy Orthodox Saint to acquire renewed strength, hope, and encouragement in our lives. We need their "holy friendship" now more than ever! We must never forget to seek the intercessions and fervent prayers of these Saints who pray for us. *God gave them to us as powerful weapons against evil*.

I suppose it might seem strange to say a Saint is a weapon. However, our heavenly friends in Christ, the Holy Orthodox Saints, do protect us. They sanctify us, pray for us, arm us against evil, and teach us how to live a Holy life. In essence, they show us how to follow God and live a Christian life. In fact, the example of their holy lives and deaths prepare us for our own eternity. The Saints are our spiritual weapons in this world in which it is becoming increasingly more difficult to be a Christian and raise a Christian family.

Instead of God being first in our lives, this has become the "*me generation*." Me first. I am a mother. I know. I see this reality all the time. Mothers in their forties and fifties are trying anything they can to hang on to youth with new fads, procedures, and injections. Love of self is the driving force. Whatever feels right in the moment works. We've stopped thinking about tomorrow. Everyone is working out the physical body but not as much working out the soul. God is an afterthought. He is only remembered during difficult times in life.

I see Godless changes coming into our world at an alarmingly speed. They are coming in through media propaganda and technology. I bet you see this too. I remember someone once telling me that what started in the Soviet Union will end up in America. He was talking about atheism. But in these rapidly-changing times, what is the most troubling is that God and His teachings are being abandoned and altogether forgotten. Not just in the United States where I live, but everywhere. Christianity and traditional values are being ignored and disregarded by millions upon millions of people. As a result, we parents who follow Christ need an *extra dose* of spiritual guidance to help us in raising our families during these times of disbelief. As a persecuted minority in many places, Christians must continue to strive to follow our Lord and Savior's teachings. He gave us His rule of life, and it is the Gospel. He gave us His life to follow.

Do we continue to remember Christ? Are we behaving as He did? I think it has become increasingly more difficult to uphold our values in today's confused world. Now more than ever, we need additional spiritual help in fighting back a world that does not think we need God. If we don't stand for our Lord, we'll lose our faith for the next generation. That's why I love the Ancient and Holy Orthodox Christian faith, its Liturgy and the acknowledgment of the *Holy Saints of God*. These God-loving Saints of our Lord are always commemorated throughout the liturgical year. This way, we always remember they are waiting to help us.

I can attest to the fact that these Saints anchor us. This is especially true when our everyday lives become confused and unbalanced. We need them as our friends in Christ to anchor us in the faith. They bring us peace as we strive to follow our Lord God.

I know this is true because the Saints have helped me many times! When I do not know what to do or how to behave in some difficult life situations, I turn to my favorite Saints like Matrona and tell them my sorrows. I ask them to pray for me. I share my burdens and joys. I talk to them when I need their help. Their lives also inspire me and give me ideas on how to get through my struggles. They show me what the peace of Christ really means.

We need to lean into these Holy Saints who teach us so much. They have already fulfilled the chief commandment of acquiring a true love for our Lord God. Many of them have been martyred for that love. No matter what, they do not back down in their love of God. They have never lost faith. They are the living proof of the reality of Christ.

They have transformed their lives and are re-made by our Lord and Savior Jesus Christ. Their lives give us hope. We desperately need role models like the Saints in this troubling age and beyond.

In this way, the Saints are our truest Christian friends. We must cultivate friendships with them. The Saints cannot do much to help us unless we sincerely desire to live a holy life in pursuit of God. When we reach out to them and truly desire to learn who they are, the start of a *friendship in Christ* takes root. After that, we study their lives and commune with them and ask for their intercessory prayers. Then an amazing thing happens: a spiritual relationship forms. *We become friends!* As a result, we begin to see good changes in our lives as we are grounded in their loving care and protection. They become our holy companions and helpmates as we journey through our lives to Christ. The results of such a holy friendship are *always good — all the time*!

It's easy to forget that the Saints are alive in Heaven, but we need to remember these holy mentors and befriend them. *Sometimes we even feel their presence.* Right this very minute, they are ready and waiting to help us lead holy Christian lives. It is especially important for us to remember that these most-perfect Christians also strive to protect us against the very real evils of this world. They have our backs. We need Saintly protection now, more than ever, against the greatest enemy of God — satan (with a little s).

It is time to introduce you to a great Russian Saint and Wonderworker of our Lord: Saint Matrona, one of my favorite Saints. She is my heavenly friend in Christ. I truly love her. I commune and confide in her. I venerate her icon. She is a spiritual guide, teacher, and guardian. I also know that she, a Saint, can and will help you. Her words always comfort me and provide hope.

She spoke straight to my heart when I learned what she said: "Come, come to me, all. Tell me about your troubles, as if I were alive, and I will see you and hear you, and help you." I cannot tell you how many times when I am faced with a worry I exclaim: "Blessed Matrona, I need help. I am so anxious with worry, please help me with your prayers!" She always said to people: "After I die, they will ask me to pray for them to the Lord, and I will hear and help everybody."

This remarkable woman who has captured the hearts of so many is: *Saint Matrona the Blind of Moscow.* Some people say she was born a Saint. She was born blind — with no eyes — but possessed the gift of spiritual vision, prophecy, and healing the infirm. It is believed that she was chosen before birth for this special ministry. Her nickname is affectionately known by many as "**Matronushka**." Matronushka said that those people who sought her intercession before God would be saved. I will never forget her words that are preserved from generation to generation. At the end of her life, she said: "All those who ask me for help I will meet after their death, *everyone.*" Who would not want to have a true friend like that? A Saint that prays to God with great boldness and fights for my soul. I know I need her!

Her grave in Danilov Cemetery has become one of the Holy places in Orthodox Moscow. People who love her visit from all over the world to share their sorrows, illnesses, hopes, and dreams with her just like they did when she was alive. Saint Matrona used to tell everyone that the world lies in evil. She emphasized that evil ways, including delusion and temptation, will be everywhere out in the open. Evil will no longer be hidden or disguised. She warned people to watch out for this evil and not fall for it. Her wisdom and guidance in the following pages can help each and every one of us not to stumble and fall in our spiritual lives.

Saint Matrona teaches us not only with words but also with the example of her whole life. Her soul was clean and free of malice. Divine grace flowed freely from her. I personally still battle with my passions. I need her help. I need her prayers. Most of all, I need her continued friendship. She reminds me how to live a life in Christ. Maybe you need her help, too.

This **blind** and Blessed Eldress shows us how we can acquire ***true spiritual vision***. She teaches us to rid ourselves of all passions that darken our minds and distort our behavior. Then we can see clearly, and Christ can live in us. It is this spiritual vision that will save us during these God-less times in which we currently live.

God gave us this warrior angel of a Saint as a spiritual weapon to protect us against evil. She will help us fight the good fight and preserve our faith for all eternity. Let us remember to call upon her at any point in our lives. From generation to generation, she will help us be cured of the greatest sickness of all, which is: *the lack of faith in our Lord God*.

Befriend Saint Matrona the Blind of Moscow, because in her, we can and will discover a **devoted and true friend in Christ**.

"Jesus Christ is the same yesterday, today, and forever."

(Hebrews 13:8, KJV)

O, Son of God, Who art wondrous in thy Saints, save us who sing unto Thee. Alleluia.

The author, pictured with fellow pilgrim Elisa Vultaggio Jackson, points out the beautiful icon of Saint Matrona with relic which resides in the Church of Saint Job of Pochaev, which is located below the Holy Trinity Monastery Cathedral, Jordanville, New York.

CHAPTER ONE

OUR TRUE AND HOLY FRIEND:
SAINT MATRONA
THE BLIND OF MOSCOW

CHAPTER ONE

OUR TRUE AND HOLY FRIEND: SAINT MATRONA THE BLIND OF MOSCOW

*"God's Saints are near to the believing heart, and are ready in a
moment to help those who call upon them with faith and love."*
SAINT JOHN OF KRONSTADT
(1829-1908)

After my mother became a widow at age fifty, she would repeatedly say, "Ariane, the worst disease one can have is *loneliness*." She was speaking from experience. Her group of friends suddenly changed. She became single. She was alone.

Today's world is currently suffering from an epidemic of loneliness. My mother would agree that loneliness is a terrible disease, a void that can only be filled by God. Trying to navigate through today's complex relationships can be quite confusing. People who don't even live alone are lonely. They are searching to find meaningful friendships.

Nowadays people have online friends, but can they be considered true friends? I think we can all relate to some of the feelings most people suffer from, feelings of some form of loneliness. They feel isolated. Maybe they feel like they don't fit in anywhere. As I moved from place to place in my life, my friends changed. I also changed. I noticed a desire for less quantity and more quality in my friendships. In addition, I did not need as many friends as before. Instead, I wanted someone with similar spiritual values and interests. The older I became I began to seek my value from God. My friends no longer took any part in defining me. God did. I yearned for alone time with God. I relished quality time in prayer. In turn, I became more selective of who I spent time with. I needed friends that could inspire me and keep me faithful to God. I began to search for friends who were more interested in God than the world. Short and simple: I longed for friends whose lives revolved around God. I guess you could say I needed *holy friends*.

Sounds like a tall order: Holy friends. I began to ponder where I was in my current friendships. My thoughts wandered to the old saying: *show me your friends, and I'll show you who you are.* I began to notice little things that spoke volumes. Some of these longtime friends were casually saying things like, "I cannot wait to see what the universe will bring me today!" These words suddenly started to bother me. I kept wanting to scream out and say the universe brings nothing! God created the universe. Only God can bring you something! I saw other friends obsessed about their physical appearances and how much they worked out. The latest fitness craze was always the topic of conversation. But what about cultivating the soul?

No matter how many injections, facials, or surgeries, a human body is going to get old. None of us are immortal. Death is unavoidable. As I got older, I began to think of my own death and wondered if I would be at peace before God. Would God recognize me as His servant? All these thoughts swirled in my head. I knew if I had a friend or two who put God first, they would be a good influence on me. I imagined I would be inspired to keep striving to do the same. But how would I find this type of friend?

I decided to pray for my desire. I am embarrassed to say I felt skeptical praying. Where and how would such a friend turn up? New friendships take time. I was already strapped by time. I tried my best to be a good wife and mother, and those take time. On top of that, I was taking care of my bedridden, elderly mother in my home. I needed time for that, too. The truth was I did not have extra time to socialize or cultivate a friendship. I truly had no idea when and how this great friend would come. I told myself to let go and have faith in God. For months, I just kept on praying. However, no new God-loving friends showed up. I started feeling downhearted. Then one day, I randomly came across this wonderful quote from a Serbian Orthodox Saint:

> "A true friend prays to God for his friend. A true friend cares about the salvation of a friend's soul. To draw a friend back from false ways and set him on the true path — that is a precious friendship. The Saints of God are man's greatest friends."
>
> — SAINT NIKOLAI VELIMIROVIĆ

Saint Nikolai Velimirović (1881-1956)

I read and re-read the quote. My heart was filled with joy because I realized I had stumbled across the answer to my prayer. It was exactly what I was searching for! God finally brought me to the understanding that Heaven and earth could intersect in a friendship! It was a new perspective to me. I could have a friend or indeed, many friends, in Heaven. A door had opened for me to have a holy friendship. After all, we know the Saints are alive in Heaven. They are alive in Christ! Saint Nikolai's quote made perfect sense!

In my excitement, I immediately decided to find one of these new friends. It's hard to admit, but I could not think of even one Saint that I felt drawn to right away. I decided to google random words and phrases like: Orthodox Christian, miracles, clairvoyance, prophecy, healing, spiritual insight, and Russian Saints. I added Russian because I adore all things Russian! You could call me a Russophile. The first Saint that popped up on my search was **Blessed Saint Matrona the Blind of Moscow.** I saw her black-and-white photograph online and that was it! Something suddenly clicked in my heart. I thought, "This blind holy woman is someone that I absolutely must get acquainted with!"

This particular Saint is one of the very first holy friends I discovered. As an Orthodox Christian, traditionally, we ask our Saints to pray to God for us. (These are called intercessory prayers.) They can help us in a variety of life situations, if we only ask them to be intercessors for us. Before my revelation, I would never have dared to think of a Saint as my friend, but now I do. Saint Matrona the Blind has now become a genuine friend. I talk to her and tell her my worries. I ask for her Saintly prayers. The unique part of this friendship is that while I reside on Earth, she resides in Heaven. It's wonderful when I meet other people that love her. It becomes a bond we share. I feel like we become instant family through this mutual friend that we commune with! As you get to know her, my prayer is that you will also become friends with her. If you decide to befriend her, your soul will benefit. I can vouch for that! I am certain this great Russian Orthodox Saint will help you root out everything in your life opposed to God and His Holy commandments. She will also open the door to hope and joy in both your earthly and eternal lives. Her prayers for you will go straight to God. She will help save your soul. You will never feel lonely again with a holy friend like Saint Matrona.

This holy woman's birth name was Matrona Dimitrievna Nikonova. Her birthplace was in a village called Sebino just outside of Moscow, Russia. Her parents were pious and hard-working peasants with four children. She was born blind — with no eyes at all — and later at age seventeen became lame. Her lifetime spanned two centuries (1883-1953). Perhaps one might think her life would have easily gone by unnoticed, however, this was not the case. She is now known throughout the world because God gave her the grace-filled gifts of prophecy, clairvoyance, and healing. She worked wondrous miracles during her life and after her death. Eventually she was recognized as a Saint.

Saint Matrona's childhood home in the village of Sebino, Russia.

Let us stop for a moment to think about exactly why the choir of Saints contains those who will be wonderful friends for us. We know Saints are people who live holy lives. They are set aside for God's service and are not bound to the world. Instead they are bound to Christ. They proclaim Christ with their lives. Thus, they have found the fountain of life and the door of Paradise.

It's easy to see that when we forget God and His teachings, we easily become confused. Confusion spells disaster. However, in the long run, Saints' lives are never ultimately confused, because over time they are able to transform themselves in His Glory. They live according to the Lord's teaching: His Holy Gospel. They become *perfected in Christ*, and that's why they become Saints! Some people claim Saint Matrona was always a Saint. In other words, one of the rare, few, who are already born — perfected in Christ. The word Saint actually means holy or virtuous. They are God-pleasers. Theirs are precious friendships for any of us to cultivate. Furthermore, it is the Lord's good will to give them to us as our true friends, friends who imitate and obey God. They know how to love, teach, and pray for us in Christ. I love it when my friends pray for me and my family!

Serbian Orthodox Christian Saint Nikolai Velimirović said a lot about how the Saints interact with us. He said they care about the salvation of our souls and draw us back from false ways. False ways are any things that erase our Lord and Savior from our memory and replace Him with worldly thoughts and activities. Too much of the world can take a person away from God. Any false way is the way of the enemy of God. It's pretty simple. If we are doing something that makes us forget God and His teachings, *that's* a false way. You know the feeling of hopelessness and feeling lost, as do I. The Saints, however, were human, but they never felt confused or lost. They could never be lost because they were never alone. God was at the center of their being. They knew how to orient the compass of their lives, even during the storms. They leaned on God to bear their crosses. I love the fact that these holy people keep us away from all of this world's confusion. Their life examples and teachings help us develop Godly discernment in our life choices. We learn from them to allow God to lead the way.

Saint Nikolai continues by teaching us that the Holy Orthodox Christian Saints are a most precious friendship to have, because they set us upon the true path. We all know that whatever is good, whatever is holy, whatever is true, is the path to God. This is where my friend, Saint Matrona the Blind of Moscow, (commemorated April 19/May 2) leads us. In her great faith, simple teachings, everyday prophecies, and intercessory prayers, she leads us on the path to salvation. This lover of God shows us how to see clearly with spiritual vision from God — not the blind vision of this temporary world. In the simplest of ways, this great Saint of God keeps us all on the *true path*. *Who wouldn't want a friend like that?*

So how do you cultivate a friendship with a Saint? First, you have to feel a desire to learn about their life and teachings. After that, you start to feel a connection to them, like one friend does with another. You place a holy image or ***icon*** of them in your home to see them and be reminded of this ongoing friendship. Icons help keep the communication lines open between Heaven and earth. As I write this book I have a small palm-sized icon of Saint Matrona next to my computer.

The icon of Saint Matrona the author held and prayed with while writing this book.

Every now and then I place the icon in my hand, and I hold it and look at it. I talk to her and ask her to pray for me and guide me to Gods will for this book. It really helps communing with a Saint when you have an icon nearby, as this holy image draws you to communicate or commune with the Saint on a regular basis. Even if you only light a candle in front of the icon, you acknowledge the Saint's presence in your life. It is interesting to note that Saint Matrona herself advised people to keep lamps lit before our icons. It's a beautiful daily expression of a Saint's aliveness.

I feel comforted when I see the flame of light flickering in front of my icon of Saint Matrona. I feel less alone when she reminds me, *I am your friend in Christ, Ariane, I am very much alive and I am here for you.* I know that there is an inexplicable reason — only God knows why — that I feel so deeply connected to and moved by the life of this particular holy woman. She is so simple, so pure, yet so wise in expressing the truth of God.

Our Holy Orthodox Saints are in Heaven working to save souls, where they hear each of our prayers and petitions. God gave each of them the job to be a Saint. We need to remember this and call upon them often! The more you learn about Saint Matrona's life and the counsel she gave to individuals, the closer your soul will draw to her. You will also begin to share your burdens with her. In time, her words will even begin to resonate in your heart. Sometimes, after prayer, a thought will randomly pop into my head, and everything becomes clear again. I feel like she whispers little reminders of her teachings. She cares and loves us like Christ. She is a great Saint that can become your great friend.

As I began to learn about Saint Matrona, one story stood out above the rest, an encounter between future Saints. It was an encounter that taught me that holy people could recognize spiritual beauty in each other. The story is about the day Saint John Kronstadt met young fourteen-year-old Matrona. He had just finished serving Divine Liturgy at Saint Andrew's Cathedral on the island of Kronstadt. When he saw her, he motioned between the thousands of people that had just attended Liturgy. He cried out to everyone to make way for her to come up to him. He then called her by her nickname "Matronushka" and asked her to draw near. When she did, he announced to the crowd with a loud voice that she was his heir, the **Eighth Pillar of Russia**. Can you imagine everyone's surprise? Even today, I often ask myself how did Saint John recognize her in the sea of people? And how did he even know her nickname? Most importantly, what do his words really mean? Could it be that he saw how she would guide the faithful Russians during the terrible years of Communist persecutions? All I know is, the great Saint John Kronstadt announced a public prophecy that day. By doing so, he recognized the holiness and importance of this future Saint. He made a proclamation about her and wanted everyone to listen and take note. Over a hundred years after his public comment, we are still remembering this encounter between future Saints. I am sure many people have discovered Saint Matrona thanks to Saint John's prophecy.

There are so many things I love about Saint Matrona that it's hard for me to know where to begin to share them all. I am struck first of all by the timing of her appearance on earth. It is said that people of this spiritual magnitude appear on earth in the worst of times. It is as if God sends us all a consolation.

Saint Matrona was born when people still openly practiced their faith and were devout and practicing Russian Orthodox believers. But not for long. As "Matronushka" grew into young adulthood, outside influences moved into her openly Christian country. The faithful were beginning to fall away from their faith and God. It is thought she was born somewhere around 1883 in the tiny village of Sebino, in the Tula region south of Moscow. The time frame of her birthdate places her in pre-revolutionary Russia, when believers had icons of Christ and the Saints in their homes and said their prayers with their families. Russia was still known as "Holy Russia." It was a beautiful land that blossomed forth churches and monasteries as far as the eye could see. Holy Russia was filled with Christian believers who openly practiced their Ancient Orthodox Christian faith. Their ancient traditions were rich and deep with sacred music, iconography, and spiritual literature. However, change was brewing. Great tragedy struck: God was out.

The new regime took over and put satan (with a small s) in. Somewhere around 1917-18 a band of militant atheists began taking over everything in

Holy Russia with their anti-Christian revolution. First they murdered the Holy Tsar Nicholas II and his family. Then they began to destroy churches and monasteries. The atheist leaders mocked religion and all faithful believers. They even changed the name of Russia to The Soviet Union. The new Soviet Union flag symbols represented a post-Christian age: the hammer and the sickle. The evil atheists murdered faithful believers in a sickening bloodbath that lasted a good part of the 20th century.

Even today, I am still surprised how people still don't see how evil a God-less country run by atheists can be. Even innocent children are open targets for them. One day a Russian friend of mine told me about how children had been targets for the atheists. Just prior to World War II, Stalin introduced a law which permitted children age twelve or older to be sentenced to death or imprisonment as adults.

This law was specifically aimed at the orphans of slain Orthodox Christian believers. Why enact such a terrible law? Because Stalin wanted to prevent these orphan kids from growing up to love God. Saint Matrona knew satan and his demons were running rampant. The God-less atheists gave them free reign. Their goal was to obliterate the Church and root out religion. Almost all clergy and millions of defenseless believers were systematically shot or sent to cruel labor camps. Blind Saint Matrona not only predicted this future tragedy, but she also lived through it. She had already seen this horror with the spiritual eyes of her soul. She warned people during this time and prayed for those still seeking God. Although

Everything connected with our Lord God — from icons to people — was confiscated and eventually destroyed by the Russian revolutionaries who were under the influence of satan.

As a teenager, Matrona foretold the martyrdom of her pious Russian Tsar-Martyr Nicholas II.

she was blind, Matronushka saw the truth better than anyone around her. God was being erased. She saw this terrible time of trouble for what it really was. People thought they no longer needed God, so they abandoned and disregarded Him. All the Russians still devoted to God had to hide their faith just to survive.

I think that God gave these Holy "underground" Russian believers a great consolation in Saint Matrona. People sought her out for help to survive and navigate their difficult lives. The churches had been closed or destroyed. God was taboo. Matronushka was not only blind, but she became lame around seventeen years of age. As Saint John Kronstadt indicated, she stood firmly as the spiritual pillar of the faith. She held people up in their own faith and erased their doubts about God. I see her as a motherly consoler of suffering hearts. As such, she guided people firmly in one way and gently with love in another, through the horrors of living in those God-less Soviet times. But God is so good. He never forgets us. The Lord gave people this Saint as a lifesaver. Saint Matrona was a spiritual gift to help believers get through those hopeless times. And now God's gift of Saint Matrona extends over into our times.

History repeats itself. Little by little God is being forgotten. We see difficult times seeping into our world. Saint Matrona was known to say that misfortune comes to those who abandon God or cease following God's teachings. The basics of life — even marriages — are confused now. With the beginning words of the Orthodox tradition of the marriage service, "Blessed is the Kingdom, of the Father and of the Son and of the Holy Spirit, now and ever and unto the ages of ages. Amen," the priest pronounces the seriousness of marriage. The sacrament is truly setting up a miniature church — or family church — by two people in order to worship God. Saint Matrona repeatedly said that God cannot be abandoned. A family works together to save their souls. This is the most important goal and labor of married life.

Saint Matrona has the reputation of being a "People's Saint" because she is so approachable. She's a Saint for everyday people like you and me. We are not looking for heady theological advice. We just want a Saint friend to help us survive our lives and achieve salvation. She teaches us the spiritual basics, and her advice helps us follow God throughout our lives. Whether we are feeling up or down in life, Saint Matrona gives us the same advice. She always tells us to pray the simple daily prayers. This includes the morning and evening prayers and prayers of Thanksgiving before meals. Saint Matrona repeatedly told people that anything we do must end and begin with God. These simple acts keep us near God as we move through our day. This is why believers like you and me must turn to Saint Matrona's counsel again and again. We must arm ourselves with the story of Saint Matrona's life and memorize her good words as weapons to carry and live by. This will keep us on the right track facing God.

At the end of this book I have included an Akathist Hymn to Saint Matrona of Moscow. I encourage

everyone to pray this regularly. This Akathist will deepen your relationship with the Saint.

In today's world, spiritual mentors like Saint Matrona are almost impossible to find. Just look around. So many individuals are confused. People don't know who or what they are anymore. Massive disbelief in God, attacks on our Christian faith, and the rejection of tradition have infiltrated our culture. We are in the thick of a God-less revolution. From movies to music, Hollywood has an agenda. You can count on the fact that this agenda has excluded God. The world and all its pleasures are all that matter, and this culminates in the physical body. The cultivation of the inner body, the soul, has no place in today's media. Outside influences keep rolling in which are contrary to the way of God. Anything goes, and no one thinks they have to answer to God any more. People are not contemplating their lives or the state of their souls.

Saint Matrona knew all about these God-less outside influences in her time. She was blind but could see the evil approaching. She told people to get ready for difficult times. She continually warned people not to forget God. Her timeless Christian advice encouraged people to repent and firmly believe in God. Repentance is our human journey of confessing our sins and reuniting with our God. Repentance is the working out of our souls' salvation. When we repent, we acknowledge God as first in our lives. The world takes a back seat. Then everything in life gets back to the correct order. The confusion in life disappears. The spiritual exercise of repentance is for the health and salvation of our souls. Repentance keeps the evil one far from us and our families. We no longer have to be the lost sheep. We find our way back to God through repentance. A sinful life, however, without repentance, can have tragic consequences. Saint Matrona understood the nature of man and the nature of evil very well. She knew full well that satan is real. In fact, she clearly saw his legion of demons with her spiritual sight. She knew what happens when God and faith are rejected. The evil one moves freely into the unbeliever's life. Then destruction begins. Saint Matrona, pray to our Lord and Savior to save the souls of everyone who reads this book!

> *The choir of Saints have found the Fountain of Life and the Door of Paradise.*
> *May I also find the way through repentance. I am the lost sheep, call me back,*
> *O Savior, and save me.*
> *Russian Orthodox Panikhida Service*

We need to remember Saint Matrona's holy life and absorb her every word. Her words always ring true. Her life work is now our primer on how to survive life in this post-Christian age. Saint Matrona often said: "Cross yourself as often as possible!" She explained that the cross is like a lock on a door and it is powerful protection against the forces of evil. She also repeated that one must always bless one's food before eating. Saint Matrona spoke simply without many words. She gets right to the point! She taught never to judge your neighbor. "Why judge other people? Think more of yourself. Every sheep will be hung by its tail. What business do you have with others' tails? Think of yours."[ii]

She also said: "Go to church, and don't watch anyone there. Pray with your eyes closed or look at some icon." Saint Seraphim of Sarov gave the same advice, as well as some other Holy Fathers. All in all, there was nothing in Matrona's advice that contradicted the Holy Fathers.[iii] During the Soviet Union days of Communist processions, Matronushka told people to not go outside. She instructed people to shut the windows and the doors tightly because she said crowds of demons were everywhere and occupied the space and even people. It is said that Saint Matrona spoke in parables, but she often reminded people to *keep our senses aware*. In other words, she simply said: we need to keep the windows of our souls shut against the evil spirits. That was true during her time, and it is true today. If your faith is alive and well, you can strive to shut out evil from your life. If a person has rejected faith and God, then the evil one has penetrated their life. They are left hopelessly defenseless and confusion seeps in. That's a scary place to be.

As my friend in Christ, Saint Matrona has a very positive influence on me. Sometimes I feel like I am a Christian in name only. She often reminds me when my eyes have become closed to God. Metropolitan Gregory (Postnikov) of Saint Petersburg (1784-1860) said "we would be unworthy of the name

Christian if, waking from sleep, we were to open only our physical eyes, and not our spiritual ones, and were to think first of the earth and of earthly things and not of the Lord God."[iv] We can all agree that Matronushka was worthy of the name Christian. Her life, from birth to death, illustrates her great faith and love of God. It's easy to see that she was literally "born" a Saint. It is said she had a cross-shaped protrusion on her chest. As a child she accidentally lost the cross she wore on a chain around her neck. When her mother became angry, little Matronushka reminded her mother not to be upset because she had the cross-shaped swelling on her chest, so she knew the cross was always with her!

Although she was Russian, Saint Matrona was really born for everyone everywhere. She was born for you and me and our future generations, in difficult times when we forget God. We know that God sends His prophets, wonderworkers, and healers prior to coming ordeals and difficulties, and these are the times we are currently enduring in our world. However, God always provides for His faithful. Saint Matrona is our great consolation in this increasingly God-less world. She is here for us.

Matronushka appeared as an angel on earth. Everything she did in life teaches us how to live as true Christians. She encourages everyone to glorify God by their life. I have a little ceramic plaque in my kitchen with a saying on it. Whenever I look at it, I am reminded of the blessed life of Saint Matrona. It says: *Your life is a gift from God, how you live it is your gift to God.* Her teachings about living a life in Christ are a magnificent gift to us. Her words and life are so easy to unwrap and understand and always carry the same clear message to us about our God. ***Remember Him. Work for Him. Pursue Him. Learn more about Him. Repent and give thanks to Him.***

Befriend Saint Matrona. She will help you. We are blessed to have an open invitation of friendship from her. She sees us from Heaven and hears us. She wants us to tell her our troubles. She can guide us to do the right thing for Christ. She also said that people who sought her intercession before God would be saved. Saint Matrona promised to personally meet those who asked for her help. I love that we get to meet her after we die! Can you imagine that? Now *that* is a precious friendship!

She is a *true friend* and has already promised to pray to God for *you*. Nothing happens without God's will; not in your life or mine. You reading this book is God's will. The "People's Saint" is reaching out to us right now, to guide and keep us on the true path to Christ! She will pray and implore our great Lord to work miracles for us.

Now let's get to know Saint Matrona — ***our friend in Christ!***

"Blessed Saint Matrona, pray to God for us to keep us safe from all evil, invisible and visible."

"Blessed Matrona, hear and receive those who pray to you."

*The author with her bed-ridden Serbian mother,
Danica V. Trifunovic, who keeps an icon of her beloved
Saint Matrona at her bedside.*

CHAPTER TWO

A Cross-Bearing Life
Tramples satan (with a small s):
Saint Matrona
the Blind of Moscow

CHAPTER TWO

A CROSS-BEARING LIFE TRAMPLES SATAN (WITH A SMALL S): SAINT MATRONA THE BLIND OF MOSCOW

I had a little chat with Saint Matrona this morning because I was upset. I did not understand something. In fact, I was shocked and surprised. As I walked my dog, I passed a little upscale women's boutique. I peered in the window and saw some sweaters with letters that spelled out, **Cheers Mother F***er!** (with an exclamation point and without asterisks — each letter was spelled out) written boldly, in large hot-pink letters, across the front of each sweater. The shop owner saw me glancing in at these sweaters. She opened the door and said, "Aren't they cute?" *Was I imagining things?* I wondered. Or *did she just say those sweaters were cute?* I could not believe my eyes or ears. Where has common decency gone? I stood frozen and confused — not knowing how to respond. I just looked at her with a sad smile. How and why would anyone design or wear such filth or even think it was cute? How could humanity sink so low? Of course, some people will say those words don't literally mean what you think. But they do. Everyone is making excuses. We should not pretend these words mean anything other than what they say!

Being *sinful* suddenly has become cute and cool. How can it be cool to come short of the glory of God? Purity and innocence and respect are out, but they should never be out. The word *mother* is a holy word. We are taught as Christians to honor our mothers and fathers. That makes it pathetic and terribly sad to think anyone would wear such a shirt. It's plain ugly. Ugly words do not lead to pure hearts. They only blind and darken the soul. We know that God can only dwell in our souls when our hearts are purified. We need to say no to *anything* that darkens our souls. Therefore, we must safeguard our hearts with discernment in how we live. We must examine the choices we make. Ugly words lead to ugly deeds.

I can only imagine what Saint Matrona would say to me. She would bluntly exclaim: "Why are you so surprised, Ariane? I already warned people that satan and his demons are out in the open now." Well, that's true, she has already warned us. The filth of satan has been unleashed for all to see. Look around. These are fearful times.

Sin is so commonplace now. *Ugly words. Ugly thoughts. Ugly deeds.* Turn on the TV. Every day we are bombarded by the so-called entertainment of immoral relationships and profanity. Our musicians belt out sexualized lyrics and seductive facial expressions and vulgar body movements. Some contemporary musicians are clearly demon possessed. I have heard their dark demonic songs inviting good girls to hell because satan is lonely. These singers promote a blatantly satanic agenda. The most shocking part is that no one blinks an eye. In fact, we give these entertainers awards! We justify it by saying its cutting edge stuff. We clap for it and want to hear more. It is the sinful spirit of satan waiting to deceive and destroy our God-loving hearts. We cannot allow this to become commonplace to us Christians.

We need to really listen and look in today's world. It's not okay for us Christians to like everything. Godly discernment is needed every day in order for us to follow Christ. We must strive to amplify our prayer lives. Families need to pray together on a daily basis. Matronushka was blind to this world, but she absolutely knew what the unseen spiritual world looked like. She clearly stated that evil spirits are real. Many times, she would read the prayers of exorcism over people, and people would become healed of their demonical influence. She especially loved to read Psalm 90. Sprinkling holy water on her visitors was routine business for Matrona. She instructed everyone to cross themselves as frequently as possible. Many people and families started going to Church and partaking of holy sacraments after visiting Matrona. I can see her in my mind's eye with her firmly closed eyelids and gentle voice, waiting to greet people who came to her. Her holy and peaceful face radiated light. However, let's not forget she was a Godly warrior. Day and night, she fought for every single soul that came to her. She continues to trample satan through prayer. I trust she is fighting for my soul!

Now's here's an unpleasant subject: satan. I choose to give that name no value by using a small "s." If we believe in our Lord God as ultimate good, we also have to acknowledge the reality of the other side, which is ultimate evil. It seems to me there is a general denial of evil in our culture. We must face the truth that the devil and his army of demons do exist. Their purpose is to get us to stop trusting and believing in God. People who love God — like you and me — are the primary targets of the evil one.

Sometimes in challenging or frightening moments in my life, I whisper this prayer: "God, save me from all evil, invisible, and visible." To be honest, sometimes we cannot see evil around us. Only God, who sees all, can defend us against the evils of this world. It's a sobering thought to think we live with these challenges. However, it's the truth.

Saint Matrona talked about evil often. As our friend in Christ, she spoke about the need for us to gird ourselves against satan. There are simple ways to start. We have to listen to Saint Matrona's advice and wear our crosses every day. Christ has transformed his Cross to become holy and life-giving. Saint Matrona repeatedly encourages us to frequently use to the power of that Cross. She said, not only do we need to cross ourselves often, but we also need to make the sign of Christ's Cross in spaces around us. She said that demons flee at the sign of the Cross. Sometimes I make the sign of the Cross in or around my car. I do this when I drive and am unsure of reckless drivers nearby. I always have any of our family's new cars blessed by a priest. I have to thank Saint Matrona for this great reminder. It seems so obvious to use it, but we often forget.

Saint Matrona reminds me that the Cross is not just for use in church. Use it at home. Use it anywhere. Every time I board an airplane, I make the sign of the Cross on the plane as I enter, and all our family members cross ourselves as the plane is taking off. The sign of the Cross is a weapon God gave us. Remember satan is not going to possess someone who makes the sign of the Cross or wears a cross. Where the Cross is exalted the demons are defeated. That's why we hang crosses in our homes and in our cars and throughout our Churches.

I am so glad Saint Matrona teaches me to use the sign of the Cross more frequently in my everyday life, and that I belong to the Church that reminds us of the Cross's true meaning. The Cross says who we follow, what we believe and hope in: "We venerate your Cross, O Master, and we glorify your holy resurrection!" Saint Matrona's life pushes me to contemplate the Cross with greater depth. We know that our crosses in life bring us closer to God.

As we study Saint Matrona, we begin to see the numerous crosses she endured throughout her earthly life. They began at birth. She was a poor and illiterate peasant who was born blind. At around seventeen years of age, she lost the ability to walk. Furthermore, she had to live in a terrible time of Communist persecution. Can you imagine surviving all that? First, she could not see; then she

Saint Matrona often reminded people to frequently use the power of the Cross in everyday life. This particular Orthodox Cross was fashioned by the author's father, Aleksandar Trifunovic, and it hangs next to the Matrona icon in her home.

had to accept that she could not walk. On top of all that, atheist Communists and her own brothers were always chasing after her because she was a believer in Christ. As a result, she could never stay in one spot for too long. She even had to rely on the good-will and kindness of other people for her basic daily living needs. Just thinking of a life with all these crosses suddenly makes me feel hopeless. She must have had an incredible faith to wait on the Lord to provide help every single day.

Matronushka had the faith of a Saint. Her loving holy heart never complained. She totally trusted God in absolutely everything, and embraced her crosses by denying herself. Only God knows how she suffered through all her heavy crosses. Her life tells me, time and time again, that she lived it totally for God.

The very first Cross of her life would have been manifested with the news of her approaching birth. Her God-loving parents Dmitri and Natalia were poor peasants with many little mouths to feed. News of her birth must have come as more of a disappointment than a joy, unlike their other children. The dilemma was how would they be able to feed another child? To top it all off, at that point, her father Dmitri was sickly. Her mother was stricken with worries while pregnant with Matrona. Mama Natalia seriously contemplated sending her newborn to a nearby orphanage after she was born. She had even chosen one in a nearby village called Prince Golitsyn Asylum. We know from the Bible that God occasionally sends dreams with meaningful messages to people. Matrona's mother

Natalia had such a dream prior to Matrona's birth. She understood this dream to be a clear sign from God to keep the baby. She dreamed of her coming child as a white bird with closed eyes. This bird flew down and rested on her arm.

I tried to imagine that in my mind's eye. I believe I would have kept the baby too, after a dream like that during pregnancy. Can you imagine how her mother must have felt when the baby they couldn't afford in the first place was born without eyes? The family's financial worries had already been a burden. Seeing baby Matrona and remembering the dream must have made Natalia wonder what God had planned for her baby. If only she could have known then that her little baby would grow to become a blessing in her family! Matrona's gifts manifested themselves at a very young age when people started noticing that after she prayed for someone, they often got better. Matrona's powerful intercessory prayers worked miracles for many people. She could see danger coming. She could see people's sins. It is said, Matrona could even read people's thoughts. She always knew the right words to guide people back to God. When word got out about all her spiritual gifts, people started coming to their home. They begged her to pray for them. They also asked for her holy advice for their lives. I am reminded of the scripture "The prayer of a righteous man has great power in its effects."[v] The grateful recipients of the prayers of this righteous woman would give the family money, food, and other miscellaneous gifts, and the financial burden became a financial blessing.

Little Matrona received her name at her baptism. She was given the name of a fifth century Greek ascetic. Matrona's relative Pavel Ivanovich Prokhorov attended her baptism. He said when the priest immersed the child in the baptismal font, everyone in the church saw a wispy column of aromatic smoke above the baby. It was clear God was showing that He had chosen her. The parish priest, Father Vasily, who was revered by his parish as righteous and blessed, was also surprised. He proclaimed that Matrona would be holy. Of the many people he baptized, it was the first time he saw this happen. And, then he added: "If the girl asks for anything, come to me directly, come without hesitation and

Father Vasily Troitsky was the priest who baptized Matrona. After her baptism, he proclaimed to all his belief that he had just baptized a future Saint.

tell me what she needs."[vi] It is known that this very priest also said Matrona would foretell his own death. One night this is exactly what happened. Little Matrona told her mother that Father Vasily had died. Matrona's parents then rushed to his house to find out he had just passed away!

Her gifts did not take away her crosses; she had so many to bear. On top of that she was a threat to satan because she was always telling people about God! One fall day, Matrona was sitting near her home. Her mother urged her to come in because it was getting a little chilly, but Matrona would not budge. She told her mother that she could not come into the family home, explaining "I cannot be in the house, I'm exposed to fire and pierced with a garden fork." Natalia was puzzled, "There's no one in the house," she said. Matrona's response to her mother was, "You can't understand, Mama, satan is tempting me."[vii] Like Christ before her, Matrona had to deal with spiritual suffering. But unlike many of us, she turned her suffering into a means *a dying to herself and living totally for God* — through faith, humility, non-complaining long-suffering, fortitude, and acceptance of God's will.[viii]

For seventy years of her earthly life, Matrona served God by sitting paralyzed in bed with her legs crossed, waiting for people to come to her. The glory of Christ's Cross literally lived in her. He sent her an endless stream of needy and suffering people, and Matronushka helped them all. She used all the precious gifts God gave her in order to serve suffering humanity. Since childhood, she had possessed gifts of divine wisdom, healing, clairvoyance, spiritual insight, and discernment. The more she helped people, the more who came to seek her out. Even today, long after her death, people are still coming to her, waiting in line for hours to venerate her relics and pray to her at Pokrov Monastery.

Saint Matrona the Blind, seated on a bed. This is how she received visitors who came to her for help.

On the day of her repose, May 2, 1952, Matrona gave her last spiritual directive. She said, "Come close, all of you, and tell me your troubles as though I were alive! I will see you; I will hear you; and I will come to your aid." I pray that one day I will be one of the pilgrims who has the honor of going to venerate her relics. The miracles that are continually being reported by pilgrims prove she does hear our prayers and that she continues to come to people's aid, even now. Saint Matrona was glorified as a local Moscow Saint of the Orthodox Church on May 2, 1999. In 2004, she was universally glorified by the whole Church. She is the protectress and helper of those in Moscow and throughout the world, and it is mind boggling to think she hears me here in Nashville, Tennessee. But she does hear our prayers and has kept her dying promise.

One example of her clairvoyance and powerful intercessory prayer is cited in a sermon delivered in February 2005 by Father Valery Krechetov in his church outside of Moscow. He mentioned how when the New Russian Confessor, Saint Bishop Stefan, was about to be sentenced to a second ten-year term in Stalin's concentration camps, he cried out to Blessed Matrona while she was still yet alive: "Matronushka! Help me in my troubles!" Shortly thereafter, he was miraculously released. Before going home, he went to find the Blessed Eldress to thank her. Upon entering the house where she lived, not seeing anyone, he called out in greeting. And the Blessed One, in response, greeted him by name. "How did you know my name?" he asked. "Why? Didn't *you* call me? As you can see, I heard you!" replied Eldress Matrona.[ix] As she heard those who called out to her while still in her body, so she continues to do for us today. I love learning how she could help suffering people — either in person or from a distance.

We can only imagine how kids must have teased her growing up. Not only the neighborhood kids, but, regretfully, even her siblings picked on her. Her brothers grew up to be Communists and continued to create problems for her into adulthood. She was different than other children, but she had the peace of God with her. Her mother even commented about her, in front of her, "poor unfortunate child!" Matrona quickly replied that she was not poor but that her older brothers were the poor ones, because they lacked faith in God.

God gave her special spiritual gifts growing up that were a great consolation to any hardships she bore from people. One day, when she was still a young child, she received one of these gifts. An old man came into the family home and asked for a drink of water, which compassionate Matrona immediately gave him. When he left, he lightly tapped her on the chest, making an imprint of a cross on her chest, which was visible throughout her life. The young child knew that her visitor was Saint Nicholas the Wonder-Worker. When the Blessed Eldress' relics were removed from her grave in 1998 and her incorrupt relics examined, this raised cross on her chest was still plainly visible.[x]

God is truly wondrous in His Saints! She won over the hearts of many faithful people throughout her lifetime. She lived in Sebino, the village where she was born, for many years helping suffering people. In her early forties she had to move to Moscow to escape her Communist brothers. When she received visitors, she sat with her hands over the head of each person. Then she would bless the individual, instruct them in Christ, and pray to God on their behalf. When people came to see her, she knew precisely what each person needed. People came to her with many different problems. Some people were sick or some lost their jobs and some had unhappy loves. She even prayed for people possessed by demons.

Some people don't believe that demons can inhabit humans, but Saint Matrona knew from experience that when faith is gone, the door is open to evil. She saw they could live in humans who had rejected faith and God. By the end of each day, she was exhausted from all that she had encountered. She never complained, but only moaned quietly. Her compassionate heart empathized with everyone's pain. She was so depleted after seeing up to forty people a day that she'd lay her head on her tiny fist and could not even speak. I am amazed at the strength she had to see everyone who came to her. It's a mystery to me how she could bear everyone's grief and heartache and misery.

The theme of her spiritual work was always the same, which was to set everyone straight on the path to God. Sometimes she would renew the faith of an entire family. She literally saved souls from atheism. Churches were always closing or being torn down in the Soviet Union, where religion was taboo. Without the support of the Church, people had struggles believing in God, who mercifully allowed Matrona to be born. He knew she would endeavor to help save humanity. The Lord chose her for this special ministry.

Saint Matrona was a spiritual pillar of Holy Russia. She prayed with a loud voice and told everyone to have faith in God. She repeated that she did not answer prayers; she only prayed intercessory prayers. It is God who answers people's prayers.

Sometimes, she said for emphasis: "Matrona is *not God*! It is *God* that helps!"

She predicted the coming of the Russian Revolution. She even told people how believers would be persecuted and killed and churches would be closed. During World War II, she was often the only source of information on the safety of sons and their return and husbands who had gone off to fight in the war. To one family she would be reassuring: "Alive! Wait for him…" To another: "They've died, arrange for the burial service."[xi] Once a Communist official came with orders to arrest Matrona. She normally got her benefactors to hastily move her to a safer location when she spiritually saw the authorities coming for her, but this time was different. She calmly stayed put and waited for him to arrive. After greeting him, she promptly warned him of danger at home. She told him to go home quickly because an emergency awaited him there. The militiaman rushed home to find his wife severely burned. He arrived, thanks to Matrona, just in time to take her to the hospital and save her life. If it had not been for Matronushka, he would have lost his wife. Needless to say, he was grateful, and he never arrested her.[xii]

Matrona had several different benefactors who helped support her. She never had a home of her own. She never owned anything. She lived in the homes or apartments where she was invited. Even then, she only stayed for a limited time. One a family who helped during World War II allowed Matronushka to live with them for seven years. The daughter said that living with Matronuska was like living in Heaven. Their home was filled with holiness, joy, and was surrounded by a peaceful warmth all around. She also said that Matrona conquered all her suffering with love, peace, and patience. It was also evident that she also suffered for the torment that the Communists rained down upon faithful Russia and the Church.

Matronushka begged people to keep their faith. She knew if they did not, it would spell disaster in their lives. She always encouraged everyone to "Pray! Beseech! Repent! The Lord will not forsake you, He will preserve our land!"[xiii] Matrona knew that if we keep the faith and love God, then satan and his demons cannot touch us or our families. Her strong directives implore us to keep our faith and love the Most Holy Trinity, God, and Creator of the whole world. Matrona's advice always reminds me of the instructive words of Saint John Chrysostom, who said something every parent should take to heart: "Your children now learn satanic songs and dances...none of them learn a Psalm, which seem to them something disgraceful, ridiculous, and laughable. Hence are all evils nurtured." The Holy Saints of God repeatedly warn us about evil. Stop. Look. Listen. We need to be aware and learn to pray for spiritual discernment for ourselves and our families.

"Blessed Saint Matrona, pray to God for us to keep us safe from all evil, invisible and visible."

"Blessed Matrona, hear and receive those who pray to you."

*"Your children now learn satanic songs and dances...
none of them learn a Psalm, which seem to them
something disgraceful, ridiculous, and laughable.
Hence are all evils nurtured."*

Saint John Chrysostom (347-407)

CHAPTER THREE

A SPIRITUAL LIGHT
FOR REVELATION TO THE NATIONS:
SAINT MATRONA
THE BLIND OF MOSCOW

CHAPTER THREE

A SPIRITUAL LIGHT FOR REVELATION TO THE NATIONS: SAINT MATRONA THE BLIND OF MOSCOW

I often think of the ways the words or actions of one individual can change other lives for the better. A few words or a short story about one life can be a light-filled revelation for someone else. The life described becomes a spiritual beacon that can turn an unbeliever into a believer. All it takes is one lover of God to make a huge difference in this world. In fact, the spiritual light of Saint Matrona the Blind of Moscow, is not only a gift for Russians. Here I am, half a world away, deeply inspired and changed by her life. The basic facts are these: she was a simple, illiterate woman, born in a remote Russian village. Against all odds, she overcame a multitude of sufferings in her earthly life to achieve a spiritual perfection that continues to save souls. Her pure and childlike faith was a self-sacrificing one that bore tremendous spiritual fruit.

The Bible teaches that when a person is cleansed of sinful passions and is filled with the Holy Spirit, the presence of the Spirit produces certain "gifts" or "fruit." These include the ability to read the hearts of people, to perform miracles, and to prophesy future events… (see 1 Corinthians 12:4-11), as well as characteristics of love, joy, peace and patience… (see Galatians 5:22).[xiv] Saint Matrona's soul was so pure that God could come in and dwell in her. She was filled with the gift of the Holy Spirit which made it possible for her to see everything. She knew a person's name even before formal introductions had been made. She liked to surprise her new visitors who came to her for help by greeting them in this way. I would be astonished, too, if she said, "Hello, Ariane," the first time we met!

Thoughts, passions, and even people's sins were clearly seen with her spiritual vision. During her lifetime, and even today, she continues to be a powerful intercessor before the throne of God. I believe people who had the privilege to meet her gained faith and salvation thereby. I feel a deep peace and renewed hope in my life when I ask for her intercessory prayers for me or my family. Her icon in my home — which has a flame burning before it right now — is a reminder to me that she is watching and helping me from Heaven at this very moment. I wish more people here in America knew about her. We all need to share her story. This way we can help Saint Matrona help the Lord gather His lost sheep here on earth! The example of her life not only gives those who love her hope in the Lord, but it also calls each of us to strive for a life of holiness. Each of our souls can be transformed and resurrected. We don't have to be a monastic in order to be holy. Saint Matrona wasn't a monastic, either.

An Orthodox priest named Father Edward Pehanich once asked a very important question. He asked: *Why is it that we do not have people like Saint Matrona here in America? A holy person that can predict future events and perform miracles.* This question really made me think. We have to go back in time to the Moscow of the 19th and 20th centuries to discover an exemplary soul like "Matronushka" to inspire us. Why? Think about it. It is difficult — it is almost impossible — to find holy people like her now. She was immersed (or as Father Edward points out, "marinated") in the divine services of the Church, spending countless hours in her village church along with hours in private prayer daily. What do we devote the majority of *our* time to? Cell phones and a variety of social media, television, movies, magazines, shopping, and exercise... The Bible describes the fruit of *this* kind of total worldly immersion as adultery, fornication, hatred, jealousy, selfish ambition, and dissension... (see Galatians 5:19) Father Edward asks us a compelling question: *Which do you prefer in your life, the fruit which Saint Matrona had or the fruit of this world?* [xv]

That's a no-brainer. But where does one start?

First, we can contemplate the holy life of Saint Matrona, starting by learning every detail of it, and one way to do that is by watching the moving twelve-part series on YouTube, *The Wonderworker Woman*. The more I learn about Saint Matrona, the more equipped I am to understand how I can strive for a holy life. Her example teaches me what holiness really is: an offering of ourselves to God by communing with our Lord and Savior every day. It is knowing God. It is making time for God, putting God first rather than knowing your phone or your friends better than God.

When you are through reading this book, go ahead and share it with a friend who might not know Saint Matrona. By doing so, you can introduce them to our holy friend, Matronushka, who gently points us to our Lord. Only God can equip us to battle evil; Saint Matrona can help to save our souls. Let's make this brave and fearless servant of Christ known everywhere!

It is ironic someone who was born blind can make us see clearly. She helps us understand that we are *nothing and nobody* without God. Blessed Matronushka clearly saw the spiritual truth of everything. We are on the true path *only* when we seek first the Kingdom of God.

And yes, Saint Matrona could see without eyes! With a radiant face and a kind voice, she received all who came to her. Once some visitors came to her and began to pity her for being blind. She lovingly told them how God had already opened her eyes and showed her the beautiful light of the sun, the stars, and all that exists in the world. She went on to tell her visitors God allowed her to see the rivers, forests, the sea, and all of His creation. She knew it was God's will for her to be blind and never complained, accepting His will with love.

There is another well-known story of Matronushka conversing with God and the Saints, and we can only imagine her parents' surprise the first time they witnessed it. While everyone was asleep at home, young Matrona would quietly get up from her bed and take the family icons down one by one from their shelf in the family prayer corner. She would hold each one lovingly in her hands and carefully place them on a table. Then she would begin to play and converse with her heavenly friends throughout the rest of the night while everyone slept. She knew each Saint by name and communed with them like this on a regular basis. Little Matronushka could see the spiritual and the earthly world.

As long as she could walk, little Matronushka spent most of her time in the local village church of the Dormition of the Mother of God. This church was just a stone's throw from their family home in Sebino. Thankfully, her family was pious and came to church often. As a result, Matrona grew up going to church. It is said that she had the habit of standing to the left from the main entrance door, at the west wall. This was her special place in church. She knew all the church chants, and she sang along with the choir. It's easy to see little Matrona had the gift of spiritual vision. No doubt, her pious childhood also gave her the gift of ceaseless prayer.

*A rare photo of young Matrona, who is seated to the right
of the priest in the center of the photo.
Even in her youth, priests and lay people
acknowledged her holiness.*

Matronushka's parents enjoyed going to church together. However, one feast day when Matrona's mother Natalia requested that her father join her, instead of agreeing to go, he decided to stay home and pray. Her mother was quite irritated that her husband would not join her in church. So, Natalia ended up going alone. She was not happy. The entire church service she wondered why he did not join her. When she arrived home, Matrona noticed this and said, "You haven't been to church, Mother." Her mother was surprised and said, "Don't you know I am back and taking off my coat?" Matrona replied, "Father was in church, but you were not." Matrona saw that even though her mother attended the service, her heart was not praying.[xvi] Every time

I think of her mother doing this, I think of the many times I put on my Sunday best and drove to church but in reality wasn't spiritually there. Sad to say, my precious time with God was lost due to my thoughts. I need to examine myself and not look at others. Maybe some of you can relate.

When I crossed myself and asked Matronushka: *What is the most important point to stress if this Chapter is about your spiritual eyes, and how you are a light for revelation for all people,* I suddenly realized that Saint Matrona exemplifies for us what it means to be a faithful Orthodox Christian. We know Orthodoxy possesses the unaltered truth of Christianity. But what does any of that really mean, other than just being words on paper. Saint Matrona's life shows us the traditional and deepest meaning of Orthodoxy. Her loving heart for everyone always prevailed over personal burdens. Her devoted prayer life and faithfulness to all the holy statutes of the Orthodox Church were the foundation of her pious spiritual life. She was unfailing even in the use of the sign of the Cross. Her steadfast God-loving ministry to people sprang from her roots in her ancient Russian Orthodox lineage. Those roots were grounded in centuries of piety and godliness. The holy vessel of her body and soul contained *the Church.*

It is for that reason that even though she was a lay person, her assistance to people bears spiritual fruit. What is so incredible is that people become firm in the Orthodox Christian faith — both inside and out. They become attached to the Church outwardly and in their inner selves, they actively participate in the daily life of prayer.[xvii] Many return to the Church to partake of its sacraments. This servant of God confirms us as Orthodox Christians. She reminds us of who we really are. We have both bodies and souls.

We are created by God to be strong in our love and obedience towards Him. Our thoughts should always be with Christ. Saint Matrona inspires us to align both our outward and inward selves in pursuit of God, so we are not just doing the physical action of attending church, but we are also with Him in spirit. Body and soul in union. She directs us to give our bodies and souls to Christ.

Matronushka's unfailing loyalty to God bears fruit for all of us. When we ask her for intercession, we soon experience the results of her praying to God on our behalf. People come to her with their problems, and when God hears His faithful servant, He always answers her. Some requests are spiritual and some are physical. The only time she ever refused someone was if they had malicious intentions. Sometimes people thought she was a folk healer who could remove the evil eye or a curse, but after they got to know her, they realized she was a handmaiden of God. Upon her advice, people would return to the Church and partake of its holy Mysteries. She asked nothing for helping people. During her lifetime, up to forty people a day came to see her, and at night she prayed for them. It's almost mind-boggling to think how much of a giver she was. Forty people a day is a lot of people! You know she had to be exhausted, both inside and out, by the end of the day. Her Saintly Christian nature just kept on giving.

Just imagine how people sought out her spiritual vision during World War II. Everyone was frightened and desperate for news of their loved ones. There are lots of stories floating around about her helping families that did not know if their husbands, fathers, and sons would return or not. Or simply where were they? Matrona gave them all answers. Because of her ability to do this, we can understand that space and time did not exist in her spiritual vision. She could be spiritually present in different locations, which made it possible for her to readily inform families of soldiers' particular situations and whereabouts. Her spiritual vision allowed her to travel to the front lines to observe and pray for them. Blessed Saint Matrona, watch over and pray for us now, *today*!

Saint Matrona had a great faith. She prayed to God with boldness. No whispering here. In fact, her voice was loud in prayer. She knew God answered her prayers. She made herself known to Him. Too many times God is so far from me. My faith has dwindled because I have not strived to truly know God. Prayers become automatic and routine. I need to follow the words of the Prophet Hosea, when he says, "Let us press on to know the Lord." (Hosea 6:3/4, KJV) Saint Matrona laid aside all her worldly cares and made it her business to know God. The Lord answered her prayers because He knew her! He knew his devoted handmaiden. I believe that because she knew God deeply and truly, her prayers yielded results. And, indeed, they did. None of her prayers were routine. Each and every one was heartfelt and unique. It is obvious that God delighted in the fact that Matrona knew and loved Him. Her great faith inspires me to actively press on to know and love God, as well.

Matronushka wanted everyone who came to see her to learn to know and love God deeply. Sometimes she asked people to work with her as she prayed for them. She knew they needed to strive to possess their faith in God and change their sinful ways. She demanded that people trust God no matter what. Every now and then she'd ask a person if they thought God could actually heal them. She was testing their faith. Matronushka once ordered a person who was suffering from epilepsy to go to every single Sunday Liturgy, as well as confession and communion of the Holy Mysteries of Christ. She told everyone living in a civil marriage to get married in Church as soon as possible. She taught everyone that in order for a marriage to be successful, it had to be blessed before God in Church. Matrona teaches us the basics. It seems so obvious but look at the world today. We are forgetting the basics.

Matrona always told people who came to seek her advice that wearing a cross was an absolute requirement, because she knew the true value of the Cross and used it as a spiritual weapon. We all should follow her lead and do the same. This was the very first piece of advice I ever read of hers, and though it seems obvious now, I will never forget it. Many baptized Orthodox Christians take off their crosses and forget to put them on again. It's easy to do. Her advice is valuable. I know I need

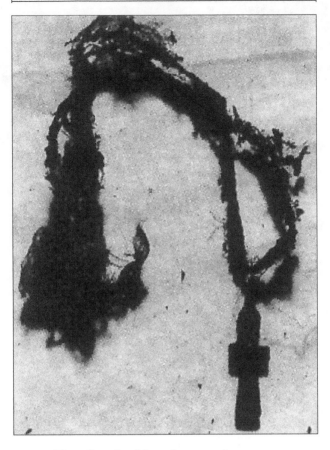

The well-used and lovingly preserved prayer rope of Saint Matrona.

these types of spiritual reminders. We belong to the Cross. It's who we are.

In the academic-style portrait icon on the front cover of this book, by the artist Elena Smirnova, you can clearly see a small indention in the middle of Saint Matrona's forehead. Those who knew her during her lifetime often described this small depression, which was created by her fingers where she had crossed herself so very often. She crossed herself slowly, carefully, her fingers searching each time for this place on her forehead.[xviii]

Matronushka liked to emphasize the following: "If the people lose faith in God, they will undergo calamities, and if they do not repent, they will perish and disappear from the face of the earth. How many nations have disappeared, but Russia has existed and will continue to exist. *Pray, ask, and repent!* The Lord will not leave you."[xix] Matrona's words are simple Godly revelations for each of us to study and live by every day. She never lets me forget that everything in life begins and ends with God. She continues to be a spiritual light of revelation for all generations.

"Blessed Saint Matrona, pray to God for us to keep us safe from all evil, invisible and visible."

"Blessed Matrona, hear and receive those who pray to you."

*You can clearly see a small indentation in the middle
of Saint Matrona's forehead in this close-up of the
academic-style icon on the front cover of this book by
the Russian artist Elena Smirnova.*

CHAPTER FOUR

SEARCHER OF THE PERISHING SOULS: SAINT MATRONA THE BLIND OF MOSCOW

CHAPTER FOUR

SEARCHER OF THE PERISHING SOULS: SAINT MATRONA THE BLIND OF MOSCOW

One meeting with Matrona changed a person. A non-believer became a believer.

Matrona was a God-pleaser. She was a courageous laywoman living in the midst of an atheistic regime, defending and guarding her holy Russian Orthodox Faith. She was fulfilling her life task to bring believers to Christ.

Matrona would tell people to make sure to pray before visiting any clergy, and indicated that by doing this they would be able to receive the right Godly wisdom from them. I guess she saw that clergy are human. Even they can make mistakes. We can all understand this. But can we also comprehend that faithful laypeople are called to be witnesses to the Truth? Each of us has the potential to impart Godly wisdom to others.

Time and time again, I have to remind myself that Matrona was a *layperson*! Ordinary baptized

Christians like myself constitute the whole Church. It's easy to forget that we laypeople can bring believers to Christ. After all, each of us is called to be a guardian of the Church's teaching once we are baptized and received into the community of the Holy Trinity. This is the teaching of the Orthodox Church. We are all called to be Saints. Simply put, we are called to be holy like Saint Matrona.

This thought always intimidates me. I am so far from holy that I have been spiritually blind in my life so many times I've lost count. I've kept looking to Saint Matrona to help me by her counsels, and pray intercessory prayers for me, for so long that I forget the obvious lesson, which is that God is calling us to be *inspired* by the life of our Saint friend. Matrona's life example shows us how to possess a *living faith*. Her life shows us ways to get through our dark, faithless times. It also shows us that everything in our life is God's will. Matrona had patience and peace with everything in her life, including her future, because she accepted His will.

Years ago, I was interested in New Age things and always wanted to know what my future held. I wish I had known then about the life of Matrona. I bet I would not have been such a confused young woman. Matronushka understood that every detail of her future was in God's hands. This realization leaves no place for astrology or psychic readings. In fact, not only do we veer from our faith, but we also abandon and forget God when we do these things. Instead, as Christians we must actively practice discernment. Trust me; that's the truth.

My Russian friend Elena told me a story that's commonly known in Russia. It is the story of a young woman who visited Matrona's grave. She looked down at Matrona's grave and all of a sudden, she heard a clear voice in her head saying, "Don't worry, I know you like to go to astrology lectures right now, but pretty soon you'll give up all of that and know God." The woman absolutely knew in her heart the voice she heard was Saint Matrona speaking directly to her. And sure enough, not long after this encounter, she gave up her interest in astrology and started going to church!

As an Orthodox Christian, Matrona was baptized as an infant in the name of the Father, Son, and Holy Spirit. The One Triune God. I was also baptized Orthodox Christian. I never stopped to think how spiritual insight or inner vision becomes available to us through our baptisms. This inner vision is how we commune with God and His Saints. I have to remember this spiritual gift is also mine. My responsibility is to work at being a Christian. I ask myself, *Ariane are you a witness to the Truth?* I love when these words are said during Divine Liturgy: "Lord, teach me Thy statutes." I have to work through the life of the Church to keep my heart pure and follow all of God's statutes. Participating in the life of the Church helps me see my way thorough each step of my life in a Christian manner. I am so glad the Church gives us Saints to emulate.

That's where my friend Saint Matrona comes into my life as a woman of God who is *entirely* devoted to His holy will. *Her whole life inspires me.*

It confirms my desire to serve God and the Church with whatever gifts God has given me.

As I write this book, my heart can feel the living presence of Saint Matrona. I cannot prove this to anyone, but I can sense her presence with me as I write. I ask her, as I write, what is the most important thing to impart to people about her life? Then I wait. I know the answer will come somehow. She guides me and encourages me as I write each word. Sometimes I wonder how I got the idea to write something that makes so much sense. Then I smile and say to myself, *Ariane, remember, you asked for her help! She is alive in Christ. She heard you and prayed for you!* When I light the flame in front of her icon in my home, I pray not only for myself but also for all the readers of this book:

"Dearest Saint Matrona, please pray to the Lord God to guide our steps and give us the wisdom to do everything in our lives for God's sake and to the glory of God."

My prayer to Saint Matrona reminds me of one of my favorite scriptures: **A man's heart deviseth his way, but the Lord directeth his steps** (Prov.16:9). Saint Matrona prays for me, but I am not the only one she prays for. I have no doubt Matrona helps every single person who sincerely asks for her intercessory prayers.

I believe Matronushka's prayers have already helped me see better. With her intervention I am using my spiritual eyes instead of only my physical eyes. Sometimes I am able to see things in my life with a spiritual or inner vision. Things I cannot explain have come true. I have had dreams that have warned me of a loved one's impending death. Some of my dreams or visions have brought me closer to God. I know by my faith and the written counsels of Saint Matrona not to analyze these things. I cross myself, observe them, and let them go. I have also sensed a living, demonic presence in certain people. Not long ago, I warned family and friends not to listen to the music of a famous alternative pop singer for this very reason. Our spiritual eyes can perceive evil where our human eyes cannot.

My beloved friend Matronushka gets me to question myself: *How great is my love and faith in God?* As long as we all live and breathe, we still have the potential to achieve a high degree of holiness. We must see with our spiritual eyes and use discernment on our way to salvation. My faith and love for God can grow — just like yours. Anything is possible with God if we truly love and serve Him.

A holy life is filled with crosses. How big a cross can you endure? How much suffering for Christ can I take on? That's a question I cannot answer, but we can see some of the many crosses Matrona endured. I sometimes wonder how much emotional and physical pain she hid inside without complaining. We will never know. All we need to remember is to trust God like she did. She knew He only gives us what we can endure. God knows what is best for each of our lives. We don't.

Matronushka shows us simple things we can all do to become holy. *Be a God-pleaser. Seek to know God.* Make it your business to learn our Lord's teachings. Christ's Beatitudes contain the most concise summary of the spiritual life of man.

Matrona knew and loved these teachings and lived them out to the letter. We can follow her lead and find room for these nine blessings in our hearts.

Jesus Christ Our Savior teaches:

"Blessed are the poor in spirit,
for theirs is the Kingdom of Heaven.
Blessed are those who mourn,
for they shall be comforted.
Blessed are the meek,
for they shall inherit the earth.
Blessed are those who hunger and thirst
for righteousness,
for they shall be satisfied.
Blessed are the merciful,
for they shall obtain mercy.
Blessed are the pure in heart,
for they shall see God.
Blessed are the peacemakers,
for they shall be called sons of God.
Blessed are those who are persecuted
for righteousness sake,
for theirs is the Kingdom of Heaven.
Blessed are you when men shall revile you,
and persecute you, and utter all kinds of evil
against you falsely on My account.
Rejoice and be exceedingly glad,
for your reward is great in Heaven."

(Matthew 5:3-12, KJV)

Do good things *for God's sake* not just for the sake of being a good person. Matrona says things like that time and time again. *Cultivate love for God in your heart. Practice your faith. Avoid evil.* These are all things Matrona did and counseled us to do. In other words, baptized Christians are called to love the Lord Jesus Christ with all their hearts. We are called to imitate Him. Let us work to align ourselves with Christ's likeness! We can please God with our love for Him. Our faith becomes great in our love for God!

We are no longer blind when we walk with the awareness everyday of who we serve. We are servants of God. Our goal is to please God with the fulfillment of our life. Our life is our gift to God. I have to admit, I need reminders of what I am striving to be. That's why I love having Saint Matrona as my friend. She reminds me to never forget what I have been given. I love wearing my cross. I love to see flames lit before my icons at home. I love the smell of church incense. I love holy oil and holy water. I love hearing the Liturgy. All of this and so much more are beautiful reminders of who I am. They whisper to me in an instant to remember I am a handmaiden of the living God. The Way, the Truth, and the Light that always conquers darkness is my Lord and Saviour, Jesus Christ. If we love and please God, He can use us — His servants — to draw more people to Him. A pure soul with a great faith is contagious! It's easy to see how an exceptional God-pleaser like Saint Matrona led — and is still leading — so many countless lost and perishing souls back to God.

Even in her youth, Matronushka was already highly respected in her village for her spiritual gifts. As a child, she repeatedly had a dream about the Mother of God. The Mother of Our Lord and Savior Jesus Christ kept coming to her in dreams to impart the message that she must commission an icon for her local village church of the Dormition. Matrona quickly told her mother about the requests from the Mother of God for an icon. She also indicated that the exact copy of the icon to be painted was called *In Search of the Lost*. Matrona even went as far as to describe to her mother the particular shelf in their priest's library that had a book with the picture of this icon in it. She insisted this was the icon to be copied from the reproduction in that book!

Her mother quickly decided to tell their priest her daughter's request, word for word. The priest could not believe his eyes when he found the icon exactly where Matrona had indicated! After Matrona learned that the priest discovered the icon reproduction in his book, she was quite pleased. She then told her Mama, "I will have this icon painted for our church." Her mother was confused with her request. How could they possibly pay the commission fee for such an icon?

Time went by and nothing happened with this commission. Matrona repeated her request. "I keep dreaming about the Mother of God. She is asking to come to our church. We must find a way to commission this icon: *In Search of the Lost*." Matronushka was emphatic. Her icon had to be completed!

This miracle-working icon of the Mother of God
In Search of the Lost, *was one of the icons commissioned*
by Saint Matrona herself.

At Matrona's directive, local village women began to collect money for this icon commission. It is interesting to me how young Matrona was deeply aware of the holiness of this commission. Additionally, she knew how to practice spiritual discernment even during the fulfillment of this icon project. There were two brothers who donated to the fund for the ***In Search of the Lost*** icon. One brother gave a ruble reluctantly. The other brother gave even less money — one small kopeck — in jest. I guess they thought it was a funny to give next to nothing for God's work.

Seeing such a lack of respect for God must have sickened Matrona. She said to her Mama, "Give it back, it's spoiling all the money for me..." It was corrupt money. She did not want these faithless brothers involved in a holy project. After all, this icon commission was initiated by the Mother of God herself.

Matrona did not want to disappoint God by taking even the smallest of coins from people that disrespected Him. By rejecting the money from these brothers, Matrona showed us her *true colors*. We can see and feel her great love and tremendous respect for God. She truly possessed the fear of the Lord. Therefore she knew the eyes of our Lord are in every place. Lord, have mercy on how often I forget this!

Matrona would not dishonor God or the Mother of God. Her spiritual integrity inspires me deeply. I need to practice her kind of consistent spiritual discernment in all areas of my life. How often I forget to do this! Matrona knew the smallest of details speak volumes. No one is allowed to mock the holiness of our Master!

The faithful village women successfully collected the needed sum of the money for the icon. Then they found an artist who could paint it. They shared their news with Matrona. However, she was not quite sure their artist could paint the icon she desired. She asked him. The artist quickly replied yes and that this was a routine project for him to complete. His response, however, did not inspire confidence. So she asked him to go to Confession and Holy Communion. He did not listen. Later on, she still prodded him and asked if he could really paint this icon. Again, he replied affirmatively and proceeded to begin work on it. After awhile, he came back to Matrona and said it was not going well. He was having problems getting started on the icon. Matrona immediately saw with her spiritual vision that he had not repented of a serious sin. He needed to repent of that sin in order to be able to paint such a holy image. Matrona told him he must confess his sin in order to proceed with the icon commission, and by the grace of God, he did. He went to the priest, confessed that he had killed a man, communed and even asked Matronushka for her forgiveness, which she gave freely. She then directed him to go back to his studio and paint, saying, "Go. Now you will paint the icon of the Heavenly Queen."

There are two amazing things about this icon. First, I love how Matrona pushed so hard for this icon of hers to be created. She was obedient to the Mother of God's request. Second: the Mother of God came to Matrona in a dream and told her that this icon must be commissioned! Wouldn't you love to see an icon commissioned by the Mother of God? It is so incredible that we have the honor to not only venerate Matrona's holy relics, but we can also see this miraculous icon at the same time!

This particular icon, *In Search of the Lost*, was very special to Matrona. It was her icon. It was painted around 1915 and, after the revolution, Matrona kept it with her throughout her life. Now it is enshrined in Moscow at the Monastery of the Protection of the Mother of God in Taganskaya, near Matrona's relics. The icon turned out beautifully, and now everyone can see it. Even today, many people continue to receive help from praying to this icon. Prayers continue to be answered! As a testimony, people leave behind gold and silver ornaments as a tribute to the Mother of God. If you visit there, you will see them attached on small chains to the icon.

There was also another important icon associated with Saint Matrona called **Searcher for the Lost**. That was the name of the second icon that Saint Matrona commissioned during her lifetime. In case you are wondering, Yes! The name of this icon sounds much like the first one! If you did not get the point of her life's work from her first icon commission, don't worry. She drives it home with the second. *Saving lost souls.* This particular icon is located at the Holy Dormition Monastery in the village of Novo-Moskovsk, in the province of Tula. Tula is the province Matronushka was from.

When this second icon was completed, it was carried from where it was created in the village of Bogoroditske to Matrona's home church in Sebino. Matrona went out with believers, leading her by the hand about four kilometers from her village, to welcome the newly completed icon and its Cross-bearing procession. This happened before she lost the use of her legs. The distance would be approximately two-and-a-half miles. That's a long way for *anyone* to walk on uneven outdoor terrain — especially if you were blind like Matrona. Again she shows us her love, devotion and respect for God. Just imagine, she wanted to have the honor of greeting the holy icon herself!

*The Church of the Dormition in Sebino
that Matrona attended as a child.*

At one point while walking, she surprised everyone and told them not to go on. She said, "Stop, do not go any further. Now, very soon, they will come, they're already close." Blind from birth — as we know — she spoke like someone with sight. She continued, "They will be here in half an hour with the icon." Sure enough, after thirty minutes the icon procession came into sight. A moleben (a supplicatory prayer service used within the Orthodox Christian Church in honor of Jesus Christ, the Mother of God, a Feast, or a particular Saint or Martyr) was served. After the special service, the icon procession continued to Sebino.

The faithful believers lovingly guided Matrona up to the icon so she could gently place her hand on it until the procession reached Sebino. This icon of the Mother of God became famous with the faithful from neighboring villages and was glorified with many miracles. When there was a drought, believers would bring the icon to a meadow near the village center and serve a moleben; after this, the villagers barely had time to return home before it would begin to rain.[xx] Some miracles were instantaneous!

When I try to picture Matrona meeting this miracle-working icon in the procession, a short phrase from the Divine Liturgy comes to mind: *Holy things for the Holy*. Matrona, the Holy Vessel, greets the Holy Icon. I wish I could have been there to see the blessed moment they met. Holiness was everywhere!

We know Matronushka possessed the Lord's gifts of foresight and healing and spiritual vision. Her life story teaches us even more. Her actions illustrate an important spiritual lesson, and the two icons she commissioned during her lifetime are part of this lesson. Matronushka pushed to commission these two important icons with almost identical names. Their names impart an important message. The message is: *seek out and save perishing souls*. This sums up for me what her entire life was all about. *Saving souls*. It is something we should all be doing.

In our own lifetime journey to discovering God, we touch many people along the way. God uses us to draw more people to Him. Unbeknownst to us, some of the people that cross our path in life are spiritually perishing. They are lost in life. They are unchurched. Maybe no one raised them to know God. Maybe they gave up on God. Just being around us may ignite a reawakening of faith and belief in God. The Saint reminds us to pray for someone we

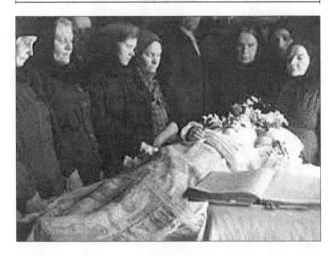

Matrona surrounded by loved ones after her repose.

meet that might be perishing. She also prompts us to pray for our own soul. Matrona, herself, can pray for our own salvation or inspire us to help someone grow in faith and love for God.

I often think that another possible title for this book could have been: *Saint Matrona the Blind, Searcher of the Lost.* This was her life theme: to search for the lost sheep of our Lord God. She lovingly sought out lost souls and brought them back to God. Not only did Matronushka gather up lost and perishing souls, but she fought for every single soul. That is what her entire life was about.

What's even better is that she is still doing it! I love to remember again and again one of her quotes that always comforts me. She said before her death, "Everyone who appeals to me for help, I will meet at their death. Everyone." Now that's love and devotion for humankind. Her desire to serve

God and help souls is everlasting. I am counting on seeing Matronushka at my end.

Let us strive to save souls. ***Our own included!***

"Blessed Saint Matrona, pray to God for us to keep us safe from all evil, invisible and visible."

"Blessed Matrona, hear and receive those who pray to you."

CHAPTER FIVE

A GREAT FAITH SAVES SOULS: SAINT MATRONA THE BLIND OF MOSCOW

CHAPTER FIVE

A GREAT FAITH SAVES SOULS: SAINT MATRONA THE BLIND OF MOSCOW

As I sit here and write, the entire world is battling the COVID-19 pandemic. We are not only fighting a virus, but everyone is also battling fear and faith struggles. We are all adrift and surrounded by rough seas.

I am amazed at the way Matrona survived the rough seas of her life. God truly lived inside her heart, and this gave her the ability to always exhibit a calm spirit throughout her life. She was a true Christian.

It oftentimes sounds easy to speak, aspire to, or write about doing the right thing. We all try to be good. We try to be helpful. We all try to love others. The fact you picked up a book on a Holy Saint says a lot. No doubt you love God and aspire to do good works in His name. A true Christian never forgets God throughout the day, the week, the year.

But *Saving Souls* is something else altogether. The individual spiritual journey of salvation that each of us endures is a challenge. For each of us, our own soul is the hardest one to save. The grief, sufferings, and emotional pain in each of our lives make it difficult for us to hold onto faith. Anguish comes in varying degrees for all people. Different times in our lives are harder than others.

It is during those difficult times that the spiritual work of Christian self-discipline often eludes me. A calm spirit escapes me. I get so easily frustrated and upset at certain life circumstances that I forget God is with me, especially when crosses in life come my way. I struggle to bear them without complaining. I lose my calm. I wonder, *why me?* I turn to God in frustration, instead of in hope.

Oftentimes, I lack patience and cannot humble myself enough to relax into accepting my crosses and God's will. After all, He allows everything to happen or not to happen in our lives. Stressful life situations occur. I begin to question things. Even worse, my faith weakens. This is where my friendship with Matronushka helps me. I try to remember her life and ask for her help.

We know she was blind, but it's easy to forget that for most of her life she was unable to walk. She always knew God was with her and had her back. As far as we know, she never questioned or voiced frustration over her life circumstances. She bore them like a true Christian. She possessed the calm spirit of a life in Christ. It's a spirit that we can all strive for. Her life teaches us how to walk the difficult path to salvation. It is a guidebook on what true faith in God is.

Try to imagine that you cannot see or walk. Both of your brothers are Communists. You openly express your faith in God to help others, and this becomes unbearable for your atheist brothers. They are afraid that because of you, they will get in trouble with officials in the Communist Party. Eventually, the friction becomes too much, and you have to move away. You leave your native village for a fresh start in Moscow. Even there, the police continue to search you out. They want to arrest you for believing in God and inspiring others to do the same. Many people close to you are imprisoned for *simply knowing you*. On top of that, you never know exactly what home you will live in from day to day.

You are the homeless wanderer. Relatives and friends take you in for short periods in their apartments, homes, and basements. You live illegally, without registration. Your host family is afraid to register you at their address. Your very presence puts each family sheltering you at risk. To escape certain arrest, you frequently have to move quickly and unexpectedly from your current temporary residence. The Soviet authorities are continually searching you out, hoping to arrest you! Finally, you have to rely on dedicated spiritual daughters for all of your everyday life needs because you have no food or possessions.

Just imagining this life scenario makes me terribly uneasy. I feel loneliness, panic, and fear coming over me. It seems unbearable. I am feeling stress, and it's not even my life! Here's the mind-boggling part. Take a moment to contemplate the fact that Matrona helped people like me. A person who can see and walk. A person who has a home, family, and happy marriage. I already have so much more than Matronushka ever did. That's what I think. **But that's where I am wrong**.

Matrona had more of the *most important thing* one can ever hope for. She had a tremendous faith in God. Very few people possess such a faith that most of us can only ever hope to have. That's why she's a Saint. She knew how to help everyone because of her great faith in God. We see how a faith like this bears spiritual fruit. A friendship with her teaches me what a magnificent faith truly is!

Saving souls. The people who crossed her path reaped the benefits of her tremendous faith. Oh, what blessed souls! I sometimes think of those forty or so people she met with each day. Her counseling each one of them was a great gift given to them by God. I often wonder if any of them ever felt they were talking to a future Saint. Each one received a different kind of advice from her. This makes sense because we are all so unique. The same is true for everyone's individual journey to salvation.

There is one particular story that stands out for me in the life of Saint Matrona. I love this story because Matrona singles out one young woman in particular, and uses her God-given spiritual vision to help this young lady change her life. The clairvoyant, unschooled lover of God helps this young woman have hope in the Lord for a bright future as an architect.

This woman was the daughter of a family who took Matrona into their home. This particular family hosted her longer than any of her other lifetime benefactors. It was a mother and daughter who lived together. The mother's name was E.M. Zhdanova and her daughter was Zinaida. They came from Matrona's native village. They lived in an old wooden house and occupied a room that was only 517 square feet. In this room, three walls were filled with beautiful icons from floor to ceiling. Glowing icon lamps hung in front of many of these holy icons. I love how God carefully arranged for Matrona to stay at homes where she was surrounded by a multitude of holy icons! Expensive drapery lined the windows in the room. Before the Russian revolution, this elegant house belonged to Zhdanova's husband, who was from a rich noble family.[xxi]

Matrona with Zinaida Zhdanova,
the daughter of one of her most faithful benefactors.

In 1946, Zinaida's father was in prison, and her mother became completely dependent on her. It was an important time for this young woman, who was a student at the Institute of Architecture in Moscow. She was about to defend her thesis project. Zinaida had to accomplish this in order to graduate as an architect. Zinaida began to feel hopeless when she realized that her thesis advisor did not like her for some odd reason. She was certain he was going to fail her because he told her point blank that her work was worthless!

In fact, her advisor told her this disturbing news shortly before the defense of her thesis. He said that the committee would surely find her work unsatisfactory. After she heard this, she wondered how she should even defend her thesis to the commission when her advisor had already made it clear the outcome was evident. What would she do now? She was hopeless and desperate after his cruel comment.

She came home to Matronushka in heartbreak and tears. She exclaimed that her only hope to care for her mother and do well in life was to graduate and get a job. Now that hope was completely extinguished by her advisor. She was utterly devastated. Matrona listened to her every unhappy word very carefully and calmly. She paused, foresaw the young woman's future and said, "Don't worry, you will pass your exam! Tonight, we will relax, have some tea, and talk about it." Zinaida could not believe her ears! She could not wait until that evening to meet with Matrona for help.

At the end of the day, they met. I love what Matronushka told her over a cup of tea.. She said, "Let's take a little trip to Italy, to Florence, and Rome, and we will see the great masters!" Then the blind Eldress Matrona began to recite the street names and the buildings. She stopped and singled out the beautiful Palazzo Pitti (Pitti Palace) in Florence, Italy. Zinaida was stunned at what she heard and made note of every detail.

The Pitti Palace in Florence, Italy.
This building is the one Matrona, with her spiritual vision, described in great detail.

Theirs was a full-fledged tour of Italy's renown architectural highlights. Matrona the tour guide calmly continued, pointing out other palaces with arches! She directed Zinaida to be sure to make note of a certain palace with three levels of big bricks and two arches at the entrance. The young woman was completely awestruck with Matrona's detailed knowledge of Italian architecture. How could she know? Not only was she blind, but she was unschooled! She realized this information was a gift from the grace of God!

First thing, the next morning, Zinaida ran to the Architectural Institute. She quickly made all the changes that Matrona suggested. The thesis committee promptly arrived mid-morning. They looked at every detail of her project and unanimously loved it. They congratulated her on her success. It was a dream come true! She could hardly believe her good fortune. She knew at once that God had opened Matrona's eyes and had shown her the beauty of His creation. Zinaida was the grateful recipient of God's blessing through Matrona.

This young woman eventually went on to become a successful architect. In her memoirs, she wrote lovingly about Matrona. Zinaida described her as an angel incarnate — a warrior doing battle with evil powers. She healed by her prayers and with holy water. She described Matrona's physical appearance as small, like a child. She said that Matrona often lay on her side on her clenched fist. It's easy to pause and imagine how she looked because we are blessed to have this first-hand account from her spiritual daughter.

I can just envision Zinaida and her mother opening their front door welcoming in all the suffering people who came from far and wide to see Matrona. Zinaida recalled that when Matronushka received people, she sat cross-legged, her legs beneath her. She would put her hands on the head of the person kneeling in front of her, make the sign of the Cross over them, pray, and then say whatever was needful for their soul.[xxii]

In her memoirs, she indicated that Matronushka knew everything that was going to happen ahead of time. Every day of her life, those who came to see her brought with them a stream of grief and sorrow. She suffered with every pilgrim. She comforted each person and healed many with her holiness. People left her transformed, their souls lighter and brighter. They were hopeful in God. Matrona prayed all night long and was often exhausted. She crossed herself unendingly. The exact details of Matrona's interior spiritual life remained a mystery even to those close to her. All we know is, above all, she *prayed*.

Matronushka continued to serve others until her end. One of those she healed did not even believe in the grace of her intercessory prayers before God. This story is a powerful testimony of faith that we can all learn from. It's the story of a brother and sister. The sister had a great faith in the boldness of Matrona's intercessory prayers before the Lord, but the brother did not believe that God was healing people through Matrona's prayers.

One morning this brother awoke to find he could not move his hands or his feet. The sister found her brother in this pitiful state. He could not focus his eyes or even move his arms. He could not even say the word *sister* when his sister arrived to see him. So, this devoted sister decided to take him to Matrona, to ask for prayers for her brother. When she arrived with him, Matrona (who had not yet met the brother) said, "Well, now, your brother says I cannot do anything, but he himself has become like a noodle… But bring him to me, I'll help." She prayed over him and gave him some holy oil. He slept like a dead man and in the morning arose completely healthy. Matrona only said, 'Be thankful to your sister — it's *her* faith that healed you."[xxiii]

Matrona shows us that a person with great faith can really help others. We can look to Matrona to help us grow our faith. We can see from Matrona that our faith is tied into the Cross of Christ. It is the profound symbol of Christianity. Matronushka was the living example of the invincible and almighty power of the Cross of Christ. A true Christian like Matrona sacrificed everything for the love of God. Her love for His people was sacrificial.

It is not a surprise when you learn that in 1925 the Lord moved Matrona to Moscow where she lived out the rest of her life. Moscow has the reputation of being a holy city. It's the heart of Russia. It has so many churches and monasteries in the surrounding area that you can literally lose count of the crosses. Matrona's intercessory prayers saved many people from their own crosses of desperation, infirmity, and death. She strived to reconcile every single person she met with Christ.

Her prayers moved mountains in people's lives, then and even now. She made it crystal clear to all that it was God who helped them. She reminded them she was nothing on her own. She was a handmaiden of our Lord who prayed a lot, and whose intercessory prayers were amazing! I imagine her praying with a bold, loud voice, as those who knew her described it, and it inspires me.

Once, I learned she even used her spiritual vision to keep herself from harm! Matrona's nephew, Ivan, lived in a place called Sergiev-Posad (in Soviet times it was called Zagorsk). One day she called him in her thoughts to come to her. Can you picture this? Her nephew could actually hear her voice in his head! He went to his boss and said, "I need to ask permission to leave work early. I can't stay. I must go to my aunt." He came, not knowing why. Matrona said, "Quickly, quickly, move me to Zagorsk to your mother-in-law." They had only just left when the police arrived looking to arrest Matrona. What a close call! It was like this many times; she would leave hours or minutes before she could be arrested.[xxiv]

Again, and again, I have to remind myself that she was a laywoman! Neither monastic nor clergy, our friend in Christ, the righteous Matrona healed people in need through prayer. This Blessed Eldress did many spiritual feats to preserve the Kingdom of God. It was incredibly difficult during this time to even find a practicing priest for any kind of assistance. Say you needed a house blessing or holy water, which could very well be impossible to come by. You would have to find a priest who had the canonical right to perform this. How could one be found in the midst of a regime of God-haters? The Soviets delighted in the destruction of churches and the persecution and death of clergy.

This atheistic regime could not stop Matrona from saving souls. She said prayers over water and gave it to those who came to her. Drinking this water and sprinkling it about protected one from a variety

of dangers. The contents of the prayers Matrona performed are unknown to this day. We know it was difficult at that time to obtain holy water sanctified by an Orthodox priest. It is important to remember, however, that miraculous healing occurs not only through small amounts of holy water blessed in church. It has also been manifested through springs and wells associated with righteous people who spent their prayerful lives near them, as well as through other springs near places where holy icons appeared. When I think of Matrona blessing water herself in those difficult times, I feel encouraged. Her praying over water reminds me that all things are possible if your faith in God is great.

In her memoirs, Zenaida actually mentions how she witnessed Matronushka's use of water. She specifically used the water she prayed over to spiritually transform people. One example was in 1946 when Matrona was still living with Zenaida. A lady in a high government position was struggling with many difficulties. She came to visit Matrona because her only son had recently been admitted to the Kashenko Psychiatric Hospital. Her husband had tragically died on the front in World War II. She was alone. She was also an atheist. She tried everything she knew of to help her only son. She even traveled with him to hospitals in Europe. However, doctors were not able to help. "I have come to you out of despair," she said, "I have nowhere else to go." Matrona asked her, "If the Lord heals your son, will you believe in God?" The woman agreed. Then Matrona asked for water and in the presence of the unhappy mother began to pray loudly over it. Giving her the water, Matrona said, "Go now to Kashenko and get the people there to hold your son tightly when they bring him out. He will fight, and you must try to splash this water on him, in his eyes and in his mouth."

Zenaida recalled that after a few days or so this woman returned. She got down on her knees and thanked Matrona because her son was now healthy! Everything played out exactly as Matrona had described. The mother went to the hospital and when they brought her son out in the visiting hall, she quickly approached him, hiding in her hands the bottle of water that Matrona had prayed over. Her son drew back crying, "Mama, get rid of it! Get rid of what you have in your hands — don't torture me!" She was astonished — how could he know? She quickly splashed the water into his eyes and his mouth. He immediately calmed down, his eyes became clear, and he said, "How wonderful!" Within a few days he was released. He left the hospital, and his health was completely restored.[xxv]

No doubt that young man's mother became a great believer in God. Her son must have, too. This preserved memory is another example that shows us how Matrona was actively waging an invisible war with the evil one by saving souls. That's why we need her *now* more than ever. There is so much unbelief in the world. It's only getting worse with time. We don't need to feel that we have missed out because she is no longer alive. We must always remember that she is alive right now. She is alive in Christ. We can talk to her right here and right now and ask her anything. *She is still saving souls today.*

Zenaida observed the actions and mannerisms of the Blessed Eldress. She also asked Matrona many questions. One question she asked was, *why is it that God allowed so many churches to be destroyed or closed in our homeland*? Matronushka simply replied to Zenaida that He allowed it because there are few believers and no one left to serve in the churches. She told her that in olden times homes were defended by icons, and lampadas were lit before them. People prayed every day. Priests blessed homes. Families went to church on a regular basis. Matrona indicated that in those days, demons could not enter homes. They could only fly near them because the homes were protected by God. But now she said, demons go inside. They inhabit homes. Matrona knew demons were real, and she had many horrid exchanges with them. She was a threat to them, and they could not stand her. She battled them often. She reminds us that demons are real.

I ask myself a question that never seems to go away. *Why is there so much evil floating around in our world at any given time?* It's simple, according to Matrona. The reason is because people have forgotten God. They do not believe in Him or even know Him. Things have not changed since Matrona's twentieth-century life. It's a replay in our time. Today's world is a world in which anything goes! I think we better listen to Matrona when she says we need to **guard the windows of our souls**.

She warns us to be vigilant about the evil one. We can sprinkle holy water frequently in our homes and also have them blessed by a priest. We can make the sign of the Cross on our front doors. We also need to light flames in front of our icons — more often than not. She offers us so many important spiritual directives like praying. There is an Akathist to Saint Matrona at the end of this book. I encourage everyone to pray this Akathist on a regular basis. By doing this, you will experience the love and devoted spiritual guidance of your new friend in Christ, Saint Matrona the Blind of Moscow. You will begin to see how this Saint can enlighten any darkness or confusion you have in your life. She will hear your voice as you call to her: "Dearest Matronushka, pray for me before the Throne of God and ask Him to save my soul!"

Matrona's advice will not only help our faith grow but will also protect us from the evil forces *that do exist*. We can employ the power of the Cross of Christ each day in different ways. Matrona shows us by making the sign of the Cross over ourselves, we are ready to carry the Cross of Christ without complaint. We are to be accepting of our life circumstances, calm and joyful because we want to share in His suffering for His sake.

Matrona used the sign of the Cross as a weapon over herself with faith and piety. She understood the Cross. She knew it was no mere talisman. When she tells us to wear a cross everyday, it is a serious directive from her. She lived every moment of her life knowing the full meaning of the Cross of Christ. Her difficult life shows us how the Cross increases spiritual gifts and virtues. She always advised people that the power and strength of the Cross dispels *every snare of the devil*. Thank God for that!

The Cross and the sign of the Cross are external expressions of what is inside the heart of a true Christian. Matrona's heart was filled with tremendous humility, faith, and hope in the Lord. She understood that each Cross bearing the image of the Crucified Savior simply represented the conquering of death. For without the Lord God, there is no life. The soul has no life. We have no life. Matrona knew that the Cross is our life-saver.

In fact, it's easy to see Matrona's life was a tangible and visible form of the invincible Cross. We must remember the evil one is *death*, and the Cross of Christ is *life*. It preserves our souls and bodies from all evil, visible and invisible. It is a weapon of the Holy Truth of Christ.

Matrona deeply understood the Life-giving power of the Cross. She used it every day and told everyone she met to use it. It is said the demonic hosts tremble when they see the Cross. We know that by the Cross, the kingdom of hell was destroyed. Matrona always emphasized that demons don't dare draw near anyone who is guarded by the Cross.

If we look deeper at the symbol of the Cross, we can grow spiritually. The Cross tells us everything we need to know about God and ourselves. The Cross sums up Matrona's entire life and teaching. Let us follow her lead and grow in faith through the mighty Cross of Christ. As a result, we will gain eternal blessedness. It continues to amaze me that a great faith like Matrona's continues to save souls in Christ from generation to generation.

"Blessed Saint Matrona, pray to God for us to keep us safe from all evil, invisible and visible."

"Blessed Matrona, hear and receive those who pray to you."

CHAPTER SIX

MATRONUSHKA WILL HELP YOU: SAINT MATRONA THE BLIND OF MOSCOW

CHAPTER SIX

MATRONUSHKA WILL HELP YOU: SAINT MATRONA THE BLIND OF MOSCOW

Matronushka is our friend in Christ. Are *you* convinced that she is *your* friend in Christ? Will *you* allow her to help *you* grow in *your* faith for our Lord and Savior Jesus Christ? Will *you* ask her for help when you are struggling?

When people read a book like this, they often feel inspired for a moment. They feel heartfelt emotion for the Saint for a short time. But as time passes, we shelf a book like this and never think of it again. I am certain this is not what Saint Matrona desires.

Long after her death, many people still dream of her. Even people who have never heard of her, dream of her. When they see her icon or photograph, they recognize her and exclaim *that's the woman I dreamt of*!

Even in our dreams, Matrona constantly teaches us to trust in the will of God for everything. In good times and bad times, she is there to guide us along the straight and narrow way that leads to Christ. ***That's her job as a Saint.*** She works tirelessly to help us achieve eternal life in Christ. Our great Lord wants all of His creation to be with Him!

In my research for my previous book, I came across a story I will never forget. The book is called *Debt of Love*, and it is about Tsar-Martyr Nicholas II, who was canonized in Russia in 2000. The story I read proved to me that the Saints are truly alive and are working for us.

This particular story illustrates for us that God acknowledges and honors His servants when they are glorified as Saints. The story revolves around a devout Orthodox Christian named Brother Basil. Brother Basil knew and deeply loved Russian Archbishop Leonty of Chile (1907-1971). Archbishop Leonty was his spiritual father.

Throughout Archbishop Leonty's life, he shared his great heartfelt love for Tsar Nicholas II of Russia with everyone he knew. He remembered how the Tsar once visited his hometown. Archbishop Leonty was deeply touched when he saw the unearthly glance of the pious future Tsar-Martyr. He never forgot this encounter his entire life. He must have immediately recognized in him a great holiness.

Brother Basil, who loved and respected Archbishop Leonty, was once granted an incredible vision of him after his death. The vision took place in 1971 on the very day the Council of Bishops commenced the glorification of the New Martyrs of Russia. At the exact moment of Brother Basil's vision, the process of confirming Tsar Nicholas II and the other New Martyrs of Russia as Saints

*Righteous Archbishop Leonty (1907-1971),
appeared to his spiritual son, Brother Basil, in a magnificent
vision of the heavenly glorification of
Tsar-Martyr Nicholas II of Russia.*

was officially underway. While in a light sleep, Brother Basil saw his spiritual father Archbishop Leonty, who confessed him and released him of his sins. Brother Basil then went on to describe what he saw next:

"At the beginning of this dream I saw myself in a huge temple not built by human hands. On the right kliros for quite a distance was a huge crowd of people dressed in white: I could not make out their faces. Around me there was a quiet heart rendering singing, although I could not see anyone there. Then both side doors of the altar swung open and from them began to come out holy hierarchs and monks, fully vested in gentle blue vestments; among them I could recognize only Saint Nicholas the Wonderworker of Myra in Lycia. From the door near me, among the passing bishops, Vladika Leonty passed by and stopped near me, saying: 'You, Brother Basil, were called and you did come. You know we have a great celebration here today.' 'What kind of celebration, Vladika?' I asked. And he continued: "The heavenly glorification of the Tsar-Martyr!' And having bowed to me slightly he continued on his way to the kathedra (in the center of the church).

"Finally, the holy doors of the altar opened, and out of them came the Tsar-Martyr, looking just as he appears in his official portraits during the first years of his reign — that is, very young. He was dressed in the Tsar's royal mantle, as during his coronation, and he wore the emperor's crown on his head. In his hands he held a large cross, and on his pale face I noticed a slight wound, either from a bullet or some blow. He passed by me at an even pace, descended the step of the ambo, and went into the center of the church. As he neared the kathedra, the singing increased in volume, and when his foot touched the step of the kathedra, it became so loud that it seemed that a whole world of people had gathered and were singing in one breath."[xxvi]

This heavenly vision illustrates how the Saints themselves are honored not only on Earth but in Heaven. We honor these powerful intercessors and protectors. If we respectfully remember them, they will also remember us.

After Brother Basil awoke from his vision, for a long time he was shaken by what he had experienced and seen. I would be shaken up, too! Brother Basil experienced a holy event that illustrates for us how important Saints are. They are even honored in Heaven! That's another reason we cannot forget about them.

We know life gets busy, and when it does, excuses are easy. Why would a Saint I don't even know want to help *me*? Maybe someone thinks *Matrona only helps Russian people*. Another even better excuse is that *miracles don't happen to me*. These and other thoughts stop us from pursuing the Saints. We must pursue the Saints in faith and love because they will help us stay on the true path. Let's face it — *life is not easy*. Saints like Matrona help us rise above worldly matters and survive our lives. Matronushka keeps us rooted in God.

Time and time again, Saint Matrona asked people *if you receive this healing or miracle will you believe in God*? She waited for the answer. She is still waiting for our response. Do we believe in God and hope in Him alone? Do we have a great faith? Are we stuck? She will help us survive our lives in Christ. We can all use the Akathist prayer to Saint Matrona at the end of this book to develop a relationship with her. Just reading this book has opened a spiritual door for you to develop a friendship with this Saint.

There is a reason why Matronushka is known by those who love her as the ***People's Saint***. A Russian Orthodox priest once said *people don't go to an empty well for water*. He continued by saying *people seek out Matronushka because she helps*! We can talk to her in everyday words and use everyday prayers. In return, we will feel her love and experience her help.

Long after her death, people who have befriended Christ-loving Matronushka are experiencing deep spiritual connections with her. She responds to each of their requests from her heavenly abode. She keeps her steadfast promise to believers by helping those who call upon her. She loves to help people, and *that's* the reason why she is called the People's Saint.

We already know that her last documented spiritual directive was "Come close, *all of you*, and tell me your troubles as though I were alive! I will see you; I will hear you; and *I will come to your aid.*" I know the first time I read those words, I thought, *I am going to take you up on that offer. I am going to tell you my earthly troubles because often I get stuck and cannot see the big picture!*

Matrona's spiritual vision was always fixed on Heaven — not on earthly cares. She did not focus on her material needs. She advised everyone to do the same. Because she always turned to God, she was able to see things that most of us cannot. Therefore, we should never despair in our problems and sadness. According to our faith, *if we ask, Saints like Matrona always help us*!

From her childhood, Matrona prayed continually. Her prayers to God helped people triumph over disease and regain strength in sorrow. Because of this inner spiritual vision, she became a messenger of oftentimes life-changing news. Her sole intention was to guide people back to the Lord. Blessed Matronushka is still helping to guide us in our lives to this very day.

Matrona always helps. People who love Saint Matrona the Blind of Moscow all agree on one thing; that God is wondrous in His Saints! If you turn to Matronushka with faith, love, and respect, she always helps! People who love her, talk to her like a true friend. It amazes me how so many Russians include her in their everyday lives as though she is a family member.

Here is one example of a mother whose deep and familiar love for Matronushka is tremendously inspiring. It is the story of Julia, who resides in Minsk, Belarus. Julia says Saint Matrona's prayers helped her two-and-a-half-year-old son. A few days after a terrible freak summer thunderstorm, her son began to stutter so badly he could not even say the word Mama. Julia was so upset by her son's inability to speak that she could not even bear to listen to him without crying. In time, everyone in the family became so distraught about the child's speech that they nearly stopped speaking to one another.

During this time Julia found out that the relics of Matronushka were being brought to her hometown of Minsk in August 2010. The family decided to go there on the first day the relics arrived. It was hot, but her young son patiently waited in line with family to venerate the relics of Saint Matrona.

When it was their turn in line to venerate the Saint, Julia tearfully begged Matrona for help with her son's speech. Then she bought some of Matrona's holy oil to take home. She also began to read the Akathist to Matronushka and continued for a few weeks. Every now and then, the little boy would anoint himself with the holy oil. Within two weeks her son's stuttering had subsided. The mother was positive that help came as a result of the prayers of Matronushka. Now her son is older and has no problems with his diction, thank God.[xxvii]

Another example is that of Michael of Moscow, who says Blessed Matronushka is his most beloved and dearest Saint! He emphatically states, "She always helps people." He has experienced her help in the most important moments in his life. For example, when there was a strong chance he would have to move to an area of the city that he didn't

At Pokrovsky Monastery in Moscow,
where Matrona's relics are enshrined, people wait in long lines
to bring the Saint their problems and requests.
They implore Matrona to pray for help on their behalf
before the throne of God.

like, he turned to Matrona in prayer. With her help, he found his forever home in his favorite region. He also believes that it was Matrona who helped him find good work, in a position he could only dream of securing. Even to this day, he still works there, twelve years after praying to the Saint.[xxviii]

Ekaterina Doroshenkova prayed often to Saint Matrona. In 2010, she had to take a long break from school, but then received clear help from the Saint when she had the chance to finish her last year in college. She borrowed money from her employer to finish her first semester, paying the loan back in installments over the next year.

The next semester (her final one), she decided to pay by taking out a loan from a bank, but then she was twice denied the loan. She was devastated. Ekaterina had no one to turn to. Her financially-strapped parents did not have the money to help either.

During this stressful time, Ekaterina prayed regularly to Saint Matrona. She read her Akathist nonstop when her worries began to surface. As the deadline for her last tuition payment approached, and after reading the Akathist again, she knew everything would work out. She felt the comforting presence of Saint Matrona.

A few days later, a co-worker she did not know very well, but who knew about her difficult situation with school, brought her the remaining amount that was due. This co-worker's mother had given her the money the day before, after having saved it especially for her. However, the co-worker really did not have any pressing needs at the time. She told Ekaterina, "I immediately understood: this money was meant to help you!"[xxix]

Ekaterina Doroshenkovas wasn't the only person in her family who loved Matronushka. Her mother also loved the Saint as a result of a beautiful miracle. In 2012, a particle of Saint Matrona's relics were brought to Krasnoyarsk, Russia. People stood in line for hours to venerate her relics. While in line, Ekaterina's mother heard this story from a nurse at an oncology center. This nurse had revered Blessed Matrona for a very long time and often prayed to her. In addition, she frequently went to Moscow to visit the Holy Protection Monastery.

In the oncology clinic where the nurse worked, there was a young woman in serious condition. She was dying and had two small children. This nurse felt very sorry for her. She had planned to go to Moscow to venerate Saint Matrona and decided to pray for this young mother while she was there. When she arrived at the Monastery, they gave her some dry roses which had been blessed on the Saint's relics. She carried the roses with her when she went back to the hospital, to give to the dying woman.

During the four-day trip home, these dried-up roses began to sprout fresh, living buds. By the time the nurse arrived to present the blessed roses to the sick woman, she was astonished to find the young mother was completely healed![xxx]

This is how Saint Matrona helps us; she helps through faithful people. The young woman knew for a fact that she had received her help from God as a result of Matrona's prayers. Now Ekaterina always exclaims, "Blessed Matronuska, pray to God for us!"[xxxi]

Sometimes it takes a little miracle to encourage us. A sign from God can strengthen our faith. It can also put God back in the center of our lives. Let's face it: *many times in life we are either lost or scattered sheep*. We seem to have forgotten our Master. I know I get emotionally exhausted and lose hope. I want something to happen to remind me that God is with me.

Many times, I lose hope in an instant. I feel defeated by something in life and feel a distance from God. Pleasure, good times, and the absence of hardships and discernment take over. It's when our lives take those unexpected nosedives that we suddenly go looking for our Lord and Saviour Jesus Christ. We know from the Bible that from time to time God grants us signs to strengthen us in our faith. We also know not to over-analyze these signs. We are to observe them and let them go.

I find these signs in my life and in other's lives tremendously encouraging. They help me grow in faith. Even a small sign from God helps remind us of eternity and shows us life is only a temporary journey. One small sign can be the key to remind us we are not alone. Just because we don't see Saints like Matrona does not mean that they are not with us. In fact, the story of Leonid Garkotin is one I read for encouragement time and time again.

Back in the nineteen-eighties, before Saint Matrona's relics were uncovered, suffering people were already coming to her grave at Danilov cemetery hoping for a miracle or a sign. Word was getting out that miracles were happening. Suffering people were searching for her grave.

Around this time, Leonid's work salary had been cut and his family was reduced to poverty. Despair and difficulty overtook his family. His good friend advised him to go to the cemetery to find Matronushka's grave. After finding it, he was instructed to tell her all his problems and ask for her help.

Admittedly, he was skeptical. He had never before done such a thing as to ask for help from a deceased person. However, Leonid did not want to offend his friend, so he promised to go sometime.

Time passed. Things got worse at home. Remembering his friend's advice, in desperation Leonid decided to try it. He hopped on the tram at Paveletsky Train Station and rode to the specified location. He was surprised because he rode around for a long time and arrived in a place called Cheremushki. He searched and could not find Danilovsky Cemetery anywhere.

When he went home and called his friend, the friend only scolded him for his doubts and distrust of Matronushka. The friend even went on to say that because of those doubts, the Saint did not allow him to come. This is why he could not find her grave. Frustrated at his failure, he prayed and decided to try again the next morning. This time he left on the subway.

When he arrived at the cemetery, he realized he had not brought any flowers for Matronushka. He wondered if he should return to the subway station. He had already walked halfway there in the cold. Should he return? Suddenly he had a clear picture in his mind's eye of a flower shop to the left of the cemetery entrance. He also saw buckets of flowers, and in one white bucket there were burgundy roses. One of the roses was taller than the others. When he arrived at the cemetery, everything he had pictured in his mind was exactly as he had seen it. He decided to buy the tall burgundy rose and proceeded to take it to her grave.

Leonid looked around and there were no other visitors. All he saw was one elderly nun standing off to one side. She gave him a quick but thorough once-over. As his friend instructed, he knelt down and laid the rose on Matrona's grave and prostrated (bowed reverently) in front of it. He then poured out all of his problems to Matrona and asked her for help in resolving them. Having told her everything, he got up from his knees.

Leonid crossed himself and thanked Matronushka. He got ready to leave and was still absorbed in worry and despair when the nun approached him. She gave him some sand from the grave and said: "Take this with you, son. Matronushka will help, and remember her lessons." Then she left as quietly as she approached him.

Not long after that, Leonid was offered a good-paying job in his specialty. Many years have passed since that visit and eventually his entire family — including grandchildren — grew to love Saint Matrona. They all visit her resting place and share their joys and sorrows with her. They also firmly believe that she sees, hears, instructs, and prays for their health and well-being. Leonid says from time to time Saint Matrona reminds them of that lesson from a quarter of a century before!

He said that one summer he, his daughter, and granddaughter were on their way to see Matronushka. As they approached the graveside flower shop, his daughter pointed out that there

*It is a tradition for pilgrims visiting Matrona
to bring her flowers from florists at the
Taganskaya Metro Station in Moscow,
as a sign of their respect and deep love for her.*

were no burgundy roses. The only roses on display
were white ones. She wondered if he would
purchase a rose of another color. When Leonid
responded that this could not be possible, his
daughter and granddaughter looked perplexed
and sad. Then Leonid asked the shopkeeper, "Are
there any unpacked flowers in the refrigerator?"
The shopkeeper replied affirmatively and brought
back an unopened package. When the package
was opened, there were all white roses in the pack
— except for one burgundy rose!

Leonid's daughter exclaimed: "Papa, look!" He said to his daughter, "It's not me — Matronushka gave you a lesson. Don't doubt, don't try to investigate, but simply believe!" Leonid's reply illustrates how Matrona had taught him to have an unquestioning faith and belief in God. Then Leonid's five-year-old granddaughter wisely added, "Matronushka loves us and is waiting for us, and we love her. Let's visit her again soon."

This little family remains happy and inspired. To this day they stand in line to visit this powerful intercessor and prayerful protectress. She is beloved and dear to every Russian Orthodox person. They see her as holy, kind, strict, and close to them. They know she is their devoted and true friend in Christ. That's why they call her Matronushka and turn to her as if she was family, and say *help us*, *hear us*, and *pray for us*!

These Russian believers — and now people beyond Russia like myself—who know her and love her all know she hears and helps those who ask. We believe she prays and rejoices, and grieves together with us! Go, ask — and it shall be given according to your faith.[xxxii]

Leonid's sweet, Matrona-loving family shows me that a love for **our friend in Christ**, Saint Matrona, can be shared from **generation to generation**. I hope my son and daughter continue the love I have for Matronushka. God knows that I have asked her many a time to pray for them.

"Blessed Saint Matrona, pray to God for us to keep us safe from all evil, invisible and visible."

"Blessed Matrona, hear and receive those
who pray to you."

*The author's children, Tony and Ana, pictured at Saint Petka
Serbian Orthodox Church, Nashville, Tennessee.
Standing between them is Father Serafim Baltic, who is holding
their family's Saint Matrona icon, which was painted by
iconographer Janet Jaime (eleousa@cox.net).
Father Serafim is an alumnus of Holy Trinity Seminary
in Jordanville, New York.*

CHAPTER SEVEN

OUR FRIEND IN CHRIST:
SAINT MATRONA THE BLIND
OF MOSCOW

CHAPTER SEVEN

OUR FRIEND IN CHRIST: SAINT MATRONA THE BLIND OF MOSCOW

This book is a personal testimony of my sincere and deep love for my friend in Christ, Saint Matrona the Blind of Moscow. I speak to her every day and light the flame in front of her icon every night. She inspires me to go one step further in many areas of my life. She has also encouraged me to develop stronger bonds of friendship with other Saints who continue to help me on my path to salvation.

I feel her ever-present watchful eye on my life. I remember when my son was in first grade and regularly attended church school. One Sunday he made a simple and profound observation. He looked at me as I tried to explain the Saint of the Day, and he said, "There are so many Saints we don't even know about, but I bet God does, Mama." I answered him, "You are absolutely right!"

Now, years later, I reflect upon how grateful I am that God has given us the opportunity to get to know the life and teachings of Saint Matrona. Her photos are available for all to see. Anyone who chooses to, can learn about her holy soul. It is truly amazing to think about the fact that the majority of people who came to see her could see and walk. Matrona did neither. In a worldly sense, they had so much more that she would ever have, but the grace of God was with her. Because of this, she possessed a multitude of spiritual gifts that most of us do not have.

Matronushka's life has become our guidebook on how to live a life in Christ. The people who came to see her were stuck in some way in their lives. They needed her guidance. They needed her spiritual vision, so the good news is that God gave her spiritual grace. Through her, He could help the spiritually blind. Then God went even further and allowed her memory to be preserved to this day. However, as my son pointed out years ago, she is only one Saint in a vast sea of Saints — some known and some unknown. They are all ready and waiting to guide us through our complex lives. All we have to do is get to know them.

For some time, I have felt a strong and unshakeable feeling that we need to have the chance to be inspired not only by Matrona but also to learn about many other holy Orthodox Saints. We need their support throughout our earthly lives. It was Matronushka's inspiration that prompted me to start The Fellowship of Saint Matrona the Blind. I thought if anyone could fight the spiritual blindness of our world, it would be Matrona. I ponder the state of the world and the following scripture verse comes to my mind: "For the hearts of this people have grown dull. Their ears are hard of hearing. And their eyes have closed." (Matthew 13:13-15 KJV)

Saint Matrona the Blind of Moscow became the Fellowship's Patron Saint in 2017, when His Grace Serbian Bishop Longin blessed its founding. At that time, I began an early series of podcasts with the goal of eliminating spiritual blindness. To fulfill this aim, we highlighted the life and inspiration of one Saint during each podcast. At the time, doing the podcasts with me was my lovely and talented friend Francene, who also participated as co-host.

I promised God I would try to do one podcast a month as long as I possibly could, under Saint

The author (second from left) with Father Aleksandar Vujković, Francene Samaras-Foster, and Serbian Bishop Longin in 2017. This photo was taken just after the Bishop blessed the inception of the Fellowship of Saint Matrona the Blind and Ariane's painting of Saint Matrona. Listen to our Fellowship podcasts of Orthodox Saints at www.fellowshipofsaintmatronatheblind.com.

Matrona's patronage. By the spring of 2019, I had gotten quite behind in taping the podcasts. So many things were going on at that particular time in my life. I felt overwhelmed. My mother was sick, my son was graduating high school, and my family was about to leave on our first trip to Europe. I had a huge "to do" list. I put my Saint podcasts on the back burner. Two months passed, and no plans had been made for another podcast recording.

However, Saint Matrona was watching me! After all, she is the Patron Saint of the Fellowship! During this time, I dreamt of her. One night, I saw a vivid, life-size icon of Matronushka in front of me. She was wearing a green robe with pale green dots on it. I had no doubt that it was her. She looked directly at me and began to speak. She said, "Ariane, you need to get the next podcast on the calendar. Go ahead, pick a date, and write it down." You can be sure, I followed her directive immediately. As soon as I woke up the next morning, I organized the next podcast.

Now, years later, I continue on as the host, sharing the lives of these most perfect Christians. I talk about the lives of these sanctified souls who have overcome death. I love to talk about them because I need my holy friends. They show *me* how to live a life in Christ. In fact, I really don't know how to live without them. They are the perfect illustration to help me remember what a life in Christ looks like. When I learn about them, I am inspired. When I speak to them, I know I am not alone. I can push forward another day in my life and try to do better all over again.

It remains my hope that more people will reach out to these holy possessors of eternal life. I hope more people will embrace them as friends in Christ. Communing with the Saints and asking them for help eventually becomes a natural part of our spiritual life. Our friendship with Saints who lead us to Christ just needs to be encouraged and cultivated!

I pray that God's Kingdom will be strengthened through the Fellowship of Saint Matrona the Blind. And I specifically pray it will be built through the inspiration of His Saints. They gave their lives for our Lord. How can we forget them? They have been sanctified for all of us. They are there for us to learn from! Their lives can help us out of our despair. They will help us save our souls!

In fact, all we have to do is look to the Saints themselves to tell us *who they really are*. For example, Serbian Saint Justin Popovich says, "What are Christians? Christians are Christ-bearers. And, by virtue of this, they are bearers and possessors of eternal life... The Saints are the most perfect Christians, for they have been sanctified to the highest degree with the podvigs [or spiritual struggles] of holy faith in the risen and eternally living Christ, and no death has power over them. Their life is entirely Christ's life; and their thought is entirely Christ's thought; and their perception is Christ's perception. All that they have is first Christ's and then theirs... In them is nothing of themselves but rather wholly and in everything the Lord Christ."[xxxiii]

When you think about Saint Matrona's life in its entirety, the Gospel comes to mind. In the parable of the blind man, Christ tells us the miracle happened that the glory of God might be manifested upon him. We see the same with the life of Matronushka. We can see she is sanctified to the highest degree.

So, what can we do? How can we be the presence of Christ in the world? How can we shine so that the glory of God is revealed to mankind through our lives? How do *we* face suffering? We need to proceed step by step in our spiritual lives. We can look to the Saints — the martyrs, miracle-workers, ascetics and apostles — to show us the way. We can always find answers in a holy soul like Saint Matrona the Blind and the many other Saints of God. *They are our treasured friends in Christ.* If you are enduring a difficult situation, then learn the lives of the Saints.

Matrona is only one of the Saints whose lives show us what true strength in Christ really is. Not only did she perform miraculous healings, but she also gave people the strength to endure hardships in life with dignity. She treated everyone with respect and dignity. Rarely did she refuse anyone's request to visit her. Why? Because she knew the value of their souls. Their souls were and are priceless creations made by the hands of our Lord God. Her heart burned then and now with love for *all* His creation.

Like Our Lord and Savior Jesus Christ, Matrona loves each and every one of us. He does not pick favorites, and neither does she. Our Lord loves sinners, and he loves those who persecuted and killed Him. Matronushka shows us how the Lord would react in any given moment. We need to take notes, because her life always reminds us to contemplate and question these two points about ourselves: Are we living icons of Christ like she was? And are we seeing the living icon of God in each person we encounter?

If I don't have time to read her entire Akathist, sometimes I quickly say: "Saint Matrona, help me draw closer to God." I light a flame before her icon. I stop and am quiet, even if just for a few moments. I look at her icon and feel a sense of calm. If I feel anxious or worried or angry, suddenly an insight will come to me and the peace of God returns. My friend Elisa sometimes talks to Saint Matrona

Ariane and her dear friend Elisa Vultaggio Jackson, who loves Saint Matrona "like an Auntie."

as she works in her kitchen. She told me that when she does, she suddenly feels the presence of a loving Auntie. I love how she describes Saint Matrona as an Auntie. When Elisa told me this, I realized something important. This is how you truly connect with a Saint. ***You connect to them through your heart***.

I look around at this world filled with noise and anxiety. Anger rages in the world news and media. In the midst of this frenzy, I reflect upon another peace-loving Saint, Saint Seraphim of Sarov. This eighteenth century Russian ascetic and wonderworker gave timeless advice when he reminded us that our main goal should be to acquire the Holy Spirit of God. In *Saint Seraphim, Wonderworker of Sarov and his Spiritual Inheritance*, author Helen Kontzevitch quoted his directive: "Acquire a peaceful spirit, and around you thousands will be saved." Saint Seraphim also taught that when peace dwells in a man's heart, it enables him to contemplate the grace of the Holy Spirit. "He who dwells in peace collects spiritual gifts as it were with a scoop, and he sheds the light of knowledge on others." Saint Seraphim's words show us how God reveals mysteries to His Saints — like Matronushka — because they live in the peace Saint Seraphim describes.

God has given us the gift of the Saints, who are our key to drawing closer to Him. In them, the help we need to endure life is graciously given to us. They show us how to acquire the peace of the Holy Spirit in our hearts, and we must engrave in our hearts the remembrance that they are our greatest friends.

They are alive in Christ and *really do* hear us when we call out to them.

One night, for instance, I was very down. I was so tired of being a caregiver for my ill mother whom I love very much. But ten years of caregiving had taken a toll. I was depleted. I was emotionally drained. I wanted to cry. So I laid in bed that night and tearfully called out to Saint Sebastian of

Saint Seraphim of Sarov's words,
"Acquire a peaceful spirit, and around you thousands
will be saved," illustrate how God reveals mysteries to his Saints.
Saint Matrona lived in the peace Saint Seraphim described.

Optina. I chose that Saint because I was reading his biography at that time.

In that book, *Elder Sebastian of Optina* by Tatiana V. Torstensen, I found some interesting advice. The Saint told his spiritual son to call upon him when in danger or in confusion or sadness. He said when we call out to him for help, make sure we state our name, where we are, and the situation we are dealing with. So, as I laid in bed about to cry, I whispered, "Saint Sebastian, it's Ariane, from Tennessee, I feel terribly sad and tired, please could you ask the Lord to give me a dream that will encourage me. I need encouragement at this very moment. Please help me!"

That very night I had a dream. At first, it seemed like a funny dream. Then I realized how encouraging it was! In my dream, I was at home sitting in my bedroom. The door burst open with the Russian leader Vladimir Putin walking in my room. He looked around the room, then asked for me by name, and I said, *here I am*! Then he exclaimed, *Ariane, look right here in this corner*! Then he pointed. When I looked where he was pointing, standing exactly in the corner of my room was one of my favorite Saints: Tsar-Martyr Nicholas II of Russia! He was dressed in military attire. In fact, I love this Saint so much I wrote a book called *Debt of Love*, which was about him and his entire family! Saint Matrona and Tsar-Martyr Nicholas II of Russia are my top two favorite Saints — after the Most Holy Mother of God.

As I told my husband the dream the next morning, he explained to me that the term, "in your corner," originated from boxing. He said that a fighter's trainer and assistant are in his or her corner. They are there to provide advice and help for the fighter between rounds. I realized its significance. Tsar-Martyr Nicholas II was in my corner! I have a Saint in my corner every day of my life! I felt so encouraged that this Saint is on my side coaching and supporting me. My heart was uplifted and strengthened. My friend in Christ was with me. The peace of God returned to my previously troubled soul.

Our holy Orthodox Christian Saints are there to help us. They are spiritual examples to follow. They are now residing in Paradise, while we remain down here on Earth fighting the good fight, round after round. Trust me, I'll need encouragement again. And when I do, I will turn to the Saints once more. After all, Christ's life continues to this day in His Church and is seen most brilliantly in His Saints. And we, too, in our own spiritual lives, are to enter into that continuing, never-ending life.[xxxiv]

I realize that each of us has certain favorite Saints. We have name-day Saints and Slava Saints. We have many other Saints we love for one reason or another. But Saint Matrona is so very special that everyone deserves the chance to get to know her! Those of us outside of Russia need her loving guidance and prayers just as much as those who live there. That's why I wrote this book. Hers is not a one-sided love. She loves me in return and loves you, too. I feel it with my heart.

We must remember one thing as we read any book or article on the Saints. *We must think of them as living — not dead.* They see us and they know our lives. They are truly alive! Furthermore, our connection to them can continue in our family from *generation to generation.* My Russian friend Elena shared the incredible story of a Russian man who has a family connection to Matrona. He recently experienced this *generation to generation* saintly family connection to her. I believe his experience proves that spiritual help is always available from our heavenly friends in Christ!

This man's name is Mstislav Kozansky and he is the great-grandson of Father Vasily Troitsky. Father Vasily was the blessed priest that had the honor to baptize Matronushka. He witnessed first-hand the miracle of the fragrant steam rising from her immersion in the baptismal font. Immediately after the baptism, Father Vasily proclaimed his belief that he had just baptized a future Saint. Of course, now we know Mstislav's great-grandfather's proclamation was absolutely correct!

Mstislav's was aware of his Orthodox family heritage. He knew many of his male ancestors were priests. Unfortunately, he was raised without any knowledge of God. Neither he nor his father were believers. In fact, his father was a war veteran who tried to join the Communist Party. He failed in this effort since there were so many priests in his family heritage. The Communists even told him, "We don't want any priests in our party!"

Mstislav was a very successful middle-aged businessman. He thought he had everything in life: a beautiful wife, children, and an impressive home. He believed he was on top of the world! In the worldly sense, he was right. His life was full. However, in the spiritual sense, it was empty. He soon discovered the transitory meaning of the pursuit of worldly success. Things do not last, and the only enduring reality is faith in our Lord God.

In 1998, there was a financial crisis in Russia, and Mstislav suddenly went broke. The financial successes that defined him disappeared. He fell into a deep despair. In fact, he felt utterly hopeless. During this difficult time in his life; God allowed him to experience an unforgettable and life-changing dream.

One night during this agonizing time, he fell asleep and dreamt of a man in a black cassock. This man was a priest. Then he watched as the priest entered his home. Once in his home, Mstislav immediately recognized him as his great-grandfather, Father Vasily Troitsky — the same Father Vasily who baptized Saint Matrona in the Sebino church.

The dream continued as his great-grandfather began to turn towards him and speak directly to him. He began to question him. "Mstislav, you do not understand your life circumstances. Why is this happening to you?"

The next morning Mstislav anxiously awoke, remembering his dream. The first thing he decided to do was to run straight to the nearest Orthodox Church. The dream was transformative. He started to cultivate a life in God. Mstislav began to go to church and started to remember God in every aspect of his life. He began to think about eternity.

Not long after this dream, Mstislav and his children were baptized into the Orthodox faith.

Mstislav went on to initiate another big spiritual change in his life, this time including his work life. He called a meeting with his employees. Instead of discussing a business deal or loan he surprised them with a building project. He told them that they were going to work together to help him build an Orthodox chapel to honor our Lord God.

What is truly amazing is that when this Chapel was completed, things immediately started to change for the better in his life. His work life began to improve. Money suddenly starting coming in, and he was able to pay off all his debts!

Today, he is the head of a large industrial enterprise. Mstislav believes that he has finally corrected the mistakes of his Soviet atheist family members who had forgotten God. Of course, this includes himself! Now, he can thankfully and joyfully say, "Lord, I believe!"

Mstislav likes to tell people, "I have one religion and it is called Orthodoxy." He continues by pointing out that the pillar of Orthodoxy is Saint Matrona the Blind of Moscow. Over one hundred years earlier, another Saint, our beloved Russian Saint John Kronstadt, described Matronushka in the very same way. She truly is a pillar of our faith!

This particular story touches my heart deeply, because the Orthodox priest who baptized Saint Matrona reached out through eternity to heal his own great-grandson of his unbelief. However, these occurrences are not uncommon in our faith. Our Saints and believing family members from *generation to generation* who love God, truly care about our salvation. Generations in a family can be saved by one holy soul. But we must be receptive. We must cultivate the desire to know and love God. The Saints will help us as we strive to do this.

I will never forget the wise words I once read from the book, *The Diary of a Russian Priest*, where the author Alexander Elchaninov wrote that, "Nothing in life is accidental. Whoever believes in accident, does not believe in God." Those words hit me like a hammer. They pretty much sum up who is in charge. Period. The Orthodox Saints teach us everything in life has been arranged by God. *God either allows it or not.*

As you read this book, you realize our blessed Matronushka is not bound by time and space like you and me. She is alive in every possible way we can imagine! At this very moment, we can stop and venerate her and light a flame before her icon. Tell her your joys and sorrows! Write her a letter, and put it next to her icon! She will read it. Speak to her! She will hear you. Read her Akathist! Call to ask your clergy to perform a service to her! Sing her Troparia! Remember to keep her icon nearby. You can have one in your home or in your car.

Little by little, day by day, you will grow closer to her. Open your heart, and confide in her on a regular basis. She will be your close friend if you so chose. Pretty soon, you will feel her presence. But, like any relationship, you have to work at it. Take a little time to be with her. Tell her your name and your specific problems and worries. Even if you only light the flame in front of her icon and acknowledge her living presence, that is a start. Then, simply ask for her intercessory prayers. I know she will be there for you.

Archimandrite Aimilianos, the present Abbot of the Holy Monastery of Simonos Petras on Mount Athos, writes: *"These close friends will be the guides of our choice and a great comfort to us along the straight and narrow way that leads to Christ. We are not alone on the road or in the struggle. We have with us our Mother, the All Holy Mother of God, our guardian angel, the Saint whose name we bear, and those close friends we have chosen out of the great multitude of Saints who stand before the lamb."* (Rev 7:9 KJV)[xxxv]

It is my hope and prayer that each of you readers will choose Matronushka out of the great multitude of Saints to be one of your close friends in Christ. Let her help you make your way to Christ! Share your joys and sorrows with her. When we stumble with sin, her prayers will help raise us up again!

As my children grow and move through their teen years and into adulthood, I remember the wise words of my mother. She'd say, "Little kids little worries and big kids big worries!" I have finally come to understand this statement of hers. A mother or father's worries never end! They only increase with time! As our children grow, we cannot always be with them. I continue to pray that Saint Matrona's intercessory prayers help me, my children, and my future generations.

Whenever my worries kick in, I turn to Saint Matrona and trust in her continued prayers, and when I do that, she comforts me. I know she is keeping an eye on my kids. I ask her to pray that the Lord keeps them safe in all ways. I trust in her intercessory prayers before the Throne of God. I specifically ask Matronushka to keep my husband, son, and daughter safe and secure on the road to salvation, and you can trust her with *your* family and loved ones, too! I truly find great comfort in my prayers to her. I sincerely believe her promises to help me, and in turn, to help *you*.

Saint Matrona the Blind is our friend in Christ.
ARIANE TRIFUNOVIC MONTEMURO

TO GOD BE THE GLORY!
The End

Thank you Lord for giving us our heavenly friends,
the Holy Saints, to help us on the path
to Salvation!

"Blessed Saint Matrona, pray to God for us to keep us safe from all evil, invisible and visible."

"Blessed Matrona, hear and receive those
who pray to you."

**God has revealed Himself to us.
Blessed be the name of the Lord.
Blessed be the name of the Lord.
Blessed be the name of the Lord.
(from the Holy Divine Liturgy of
Saint John Chrysostom)**

FRIENDS IN CHRIST WHO LOVE
SAINT MATRONA THE BLIND

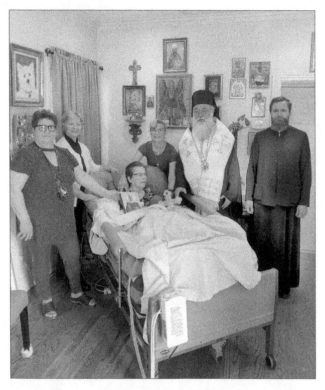

Ariane's mother, Danica, was blessed to have a bedside visit with prayers offered on her behalf by Serbian Bishop Longin. Danica is holding her icon of Saint Matrona and is surrounded by those who pray, love, and care for her.
Pictured, left to right, Milja Maksić, Slavka Opacić, Danica, Ariane, Bishop Longin, and Father Aleksandar Vujković. Everyone in this photo loves and honors Saint Matrona.

*Father Dragan Micanović, pictured here with the author and
her mother Danica and family icon of Saint Matrona.
Father Dragan is planning to bring Saint Matrona's holy relics to
Ariane's home parish of Saint Petka, Nashville, Tennessee.*

Chicago residents Sinisa and Veneta Jevtović deeply love Saint
Matrona and have visited her monastery in Russia.
In September 2017, they made a donation in Saint Matrona's
honor to the Nativity of the Mother of God Serbian Orthodox
Monastery in New Carlisle, Indiana.
Ariane was so moved by their deep love for Saint Matrona
that she gifted them with her original oil painting of the Saint.

*Muscovite Oxsana, is a regular visitor to
Pokrovsky Monastery in Moscow, Russia.
Oxsana is holding a stained glass icon of Saint Matrona the
Blind created by the author's friend Wyn Davies.*

*Father Christopher and Matushka Mary Sara Stanton
hold an icon of Saint Matrona whom they love and venerate.*

The author's dear friend Francene Samaras-Foster loves and admires Saint Matrona the Blind.
Here she is seen holding her favorite family icon of the Saint.

Saint Matrona is loved all over the world.
Stefan Radović, a Serbian seminarian who also has a great
respect and love for Saint Matrona, holds Ariane's newest book.
Her painting of Saint Sava is pictured behind them.
A gallery of Ariane's artwork is on permanent display in
the Fellowship Hall at Saint Petka Church, Nashville, Tennessee.

> *"If we exclaim, 'All Saints, pray to God for us!'*
> *then the whole Heaven will immediately pray,*
> *'O Lord, help them!'"*
> VENERABLE BARSANUPHIUS OF OPTINA

Dearest Reader,

If you love Saint Matrona and have been inspired by this book about her holy life, please consider making a donation to Holy Trinity Seminary in Jordanville, New York (www.hts.edu). Your donation will help preserve the Holy Orthodox Faith that Saint Matrona worked so hard to keep alive in peoples' hearts during the God-less times in which she lived.

Thank you and with much love in Christ,

ARIANE TRIFUNOVIC MONTEMURO
Nashville, Tennessee
January 2021

"Blessed Saint Matrona, pray to God for us to keep us safe from all evil, invisible and visible."

"Blessed Matrona, hear and receive those
who pray to you."

*This beautiful icon of Saint Matrona the Blind, with relic,
resides in the Church of Saint Job of Pochaev,
which is located beneath the Holy Trinity Monastery Cathedral,
Jordanville, New York*

AKATHIST TO BLESSED ELDRESS
MATRONA OF MOSCOW[xxxvi]

Kontakion 1

Chosen by God from the swaddling clothes, thou didst receive the gift of clairvoyance, wonderworking and healing by the grace of the Holy Spirit, O Blessed Eldress Matrona, thou wast crowned with an incorruptible crown by the Lord in Heaven; now we, the Orthodox, also weave a crown of praise on earth from the spiritual songs. Do thou, O Blessed Mother, accept this from our grateful hearts and, as thou hast boldness before the Lord, deliver us from all troubles, sorrows, diseases and enemy's crafty designs, so that we might sing to thee with love: Rejoice, O Blessed Eldress Matrona, most wondrous wonderworker.

Ikos 1

An angel in the flesh thou didst appear on earth in thy nativity; although thou wast seen by all as having no bodily eyes, but the Lord, Who maketh the blind wise and Who loveth the righteous, illumined thy spiritual eyes, so that thou wouldest be a foreseer of the future as if it were present and a healer of those suffering from diverse diseases. Therefore, we call out, O Mother, such things us these:

Rejoice, thou who wast chosen by God from infancy;

Rejoice, thou who wast illumined by the grace of the Holy Spirit from thy swaddling clothes.

Rejoice, thou who wast endowed with the gift of wonderworking from thy youth;

Rejoice, thou who wast gifted with the wisdom of God from on high.

Rejoice, for deprived of bodily eyes, thou wast enlightened with spiritual eyes;

Rejoice, thou who wast made by God wiser than those who have eyes and are full of wisdom of this world.

Rejoice, O Blessed Eldress Matrona, most wondrous wonderworker.

Kontakion 2

The priest and the people who were present at thy baptism saw a pillar as if made of steam rising from the holy baptismal font and, at the same time, they smelled a powerful fragrance in the temple, so they understood thou wast a righteous one, granted from God to earth, and they glorified God, Who worketh the wondrous and most glorious things in His people, with the angelic song: Alleluia.

Ikos 2

Having mind illumined from on high, the priest of God who baptized thee learned that the child baptized by him was a vessel of God's grace, and he called thee a holy child. And we, with all our zeal, offer these praises to thee: child, given by God as a gift;

Rejoice, thou who wast incensed by the grace of the Holy Spirit from the holy baptismal font.

Rejoice, thou who from thy birth wast named a holy one by the priest of God who baptized thee;

Rejoice, thou whose body was sealed with Cross by God.

Rejoice, thou who wast glorified on earth by the gift of wonderworking from God;

Rejoice, thou who wast crowned by the Lord in Heaven with the unfading crown.

Rejoice, O Blessed Eldress Matrona, most wondrous wonderworker.

Kontakion 3

By the power of the Most High, in thy infancy, O Saint, thou wast carried from thy bed to the holy icons and there thou wast rejoicing as if with thy friends and with the childish babble of thy lips thou didst glorify God, Who is accustomed to being praised from the mouths of the infants, singing to Him with the pure heart: Alleluia.

Ikos 3

Possessing a gift of clairvoyance from God, having no bodily eyes from thy birth, with thy spiritual eyes open, thou didst foretell to people the future as if it were present, and thou didst endure mockery and dishonor from thy relatives and those near thee when they heard of it, but receive from the faithful such things as these:

Rejoice, O wondrous foreseer;

Rejoice, O sure foreteller of the things invisible and distant.

Rejoice, thou who art endowed with the gift of prophecy from God; Rejoice, thou who didst console many with the gift.

Rejoice, thou who didst not take anything from the ailing for their healing;

Rejoice, thou who didst endure without murmur both mockery and reproaches for it.

Rejoice, O Blessed Eldress Matrona, most wondrous wonderworker.

Kontakion 4
Storm of bewilderment and confusion hath surrounded me: how can I praise and glorify the life of the holy righteous one, if not the Lord, Who is wonderful in His Saints, through the prayers of the blessed Eldress, would enlighten my mind, so that I could hymn Him for this with a song of praise: Alleluia.

Ikos 4
The people, who heard from thee, O Mother Matrona, foretelling of what would happen to them in their lives, thronged to thee with their quandaries, sorrows and grief and, having received consolation and sound counsel, they call out with

the grateful hearts to thee:

Rejoice, O good disperser of our delusions and confusions;

Rejoice, O assuager of our grief. comforter of our Sorrows',

Rejoice, O teacher of piety.

Rejoice, O good unmercenary;

Rejoice, O dispeller of all kinds of infirmities.

Rejoice, O Blessed Eldress Matrona, most wondrous wonderworker.

Kontakion 5

A God-streaming star thou didst appear, O Blessed Mother Matrona, in the capital city of Moscow as a wanderer — having no lasting city — thou didst move from place to place, bringing clarity of thought to the confused, alleviation to the suffering, healing to the sick, so that they might call out in thanksgiving to God: Alleluia.

Ikos 5

Seeing a great river of miracles and healings flowing from thee by the Divine grace: walking for the lame, healing for the paralyzed and lying on the sickbed, liberation from the evil spirits for the demon-possessed. All the suffering and the afflicted who hastened to thee, O Mother, as to an inexhaustible font of miracles, quenched their thirst generously, and being consoled and healed they cried out with tender hearts to thee:

Rejoice, O Righteous One, sent down to us from God;

Rejoice, O physician, healing all our infirmities.

Rejoice, O helper, with thy counsels bringing benefit to our souls;

Rejoice, O quick resolver of all our bewilderments and confusions.

Rejoice, O expeller of demons from the suffering people;

Rejoice, O teacher of the fight way leading to God.

Rejoice, O Blessed Eldress Matrona, most wondrous wonderworker.

Kontakion 6
Holy Father John of Kronstadt appeared as a preacher of the holiness and righteousness of thy life, O Blessed One, commanding the people in the temple to clear the way and let the young maiden Matrona come to him, calling her his successor and the eighth pillar of Russia. And all who heard of it glorified the Lord, raising their voices to Him in a heavenly song: Alleluia.

Ikos 6

Thou didst shine with thy prayers the light of God's grace in the hearts of those who did not know God and inclined Him to wrath with their many sins; but seeing the miracles wrought by thee, they turned to the Lord, magnifying the Blessed Eldress with these doxologies:

Rejoice, O thou who glorifiest God with thy miracles;

Rejoice, O thou who disclosest to us the majesty of God and His glory in them.

Rejoice, O thou who turnest the souls of the unbelievers to God; thou who enlightenest with the light of God the souls darkened by unbelief.

Rejoice, O thou who teachest us repentance and commandments of God;

Rejoice, O thou who exhortest us to offer glory and thanksgiving to the Lord for everything.

Rejoice, O Blessed Eldress Matrona, most wondrous wonderworker.

Kontakion 7

Desiring to save His creation in these latter times, when all the power of the enemy, for apostasy from God and unrepentiveness in numerous sins, rose against God's creation, the merciful Lord sendeth His faithful servants into the sinful world, and

Blessed Eldress Matrona was revealed as such an ascetic and supplicant before God. Therefore, let us glorify God's tenderheartedness towards us sinners, singing to Him in gratitude: Alleluia.

Ikos 7

The Lord has granted to people of Russia a new and wondrous intercessor, supplicant, physician and mediator for them before God after the Elders of Optina Hermitage: Leo, Makary and Amvrosy, and Holy Righteous John of Kronstadt had departed this world, and He teacheth all to sing to His faithful servant Blessed Eldress Matrona such things as these:

Rejoice, O intercessor for our salvation before God;

Rejoice, O propitiator of the Righteous Judge for the forgiveness of our sins.

Rejoice, O diligent visitor of holy churches and monasteries;

Rejoice, O God-sent protector of the helpless and the hopelessly sick and the wronged.

Rejoice, O untiring warrior against the hosts of demons and their crafty designs; Rejoice, O Christ's bloodless martyr, the conqueror of the devil — most evil torturer.

Rejoice, O Blessed Eldress Matrona, most wondrous wonderworker.

Kontakion 8

A strange wonder it was to the unbelievers and those without understanding how a blind can see and know not only the present, but even the future, for they did not know the power of God working in the human frailty nor how to sing to God: Alleluia.

Ikos 8

Thou wast fully in God, O Saint, even if thou wast bodily in this sinful world; being always surrounded by believers and unbelievers, pious and impious, thou didst not reject anyone, but didst offer them sympathy and consolation, while enduring vexation and wrongdoings, persecutions, sorrows and reproaches; yet, thou didst not complain about it, but didst thank God for everything, thus encouraging us to bear our cross patiently. Therefore, we offer her such praises as these:

Rejoice, thou who didst endure many sorrows and afflictions for healing of the infirm;

Rejoice, thou who wast spending all thy life fighting against the foul spirits. Rejoice, thou who wast robbed by evil people of the ability to walk for this;

Rejoice, thou who wast ceaselessly in fervent prayer.

Rejoice, thou who didst lean thy head on thy fist and thus sitting thou tookest thy rest;

Rejoice, thou who didst spend all nights in prayer with alert spirit.

Rejoice, O Blessed Eldress Matrona, most wondrous wonderworker.

Kontakion 9
Thou didst endure diverse sorrows and diseases, O Mother Matrona, ceaselessly fighting the powers of darkness, driving them away from those possessed by the unclean spirits, exposing their wicked designs and craftiness, and thou didst never murmur but till thy death didst thou help the suffering, ailing and sorrowful, ever singing to the Lord God, Who giveth thee His strength: Alleluia.

Ikos 9
Eloquent orators are not able to rightly understand the gifts of the grace of the Holy Spirit from on high given to thee by God, neither can they describe nor glorify all holiness of thy life and the miracles thou wrought by the power of God. Moreover, how can we, blinded in our spiritual eyes, comprehend the plans of God fulfilled on thee and, with the sinful lips, how can we sing and glorify thee, O Blessed Mother? But desiring, according to the words of the Psalmist, to praise God in His Saints, we are exalted by our heartfelt love to thee and dare offer thee this praise and call to thee:

Rejoice, O poor in spirit, for to such belongeth the Kingdom of Heaven;

Rejoice, thou who didst walk the narrow and thorny way.

Rejoice, thou who didst fly from place to place like a bird;

Rejoice, for if the birds of Heaven have nests, thou didst not acquire a home, nor treasures on earth.

Rejoice, for to the Son of God, Who had no place where to lay His head, thou didst liken thyself on earth;

Rejoice, for today thou dwellest in the paradisiacal abodes in Heaven with Him.

Rejoice, O Blessed Eldress Matrona, most wondrous wonderworker.

Kontakion 10
Desiring to save many people from bodily sufferings and afflictions of their souls, thou, O Righteous One of God, didst spend all nights in prayer on bended knees, asking for help and strength from Our Lord Jesus Christ Who, during His earthly sojourn, bent His knees in prayer before the Heavenly Father, singing together with the angels to Him: Alleluia.

Ikos 10
A wall and protection wast thou in thy life, O Blessed Mother, to all those fleeing to thee in difficult circumstances and sorrows, but also after thy death thou didst not cease to intercede before God for us who come to thee with faith. Now, O Good Mother, hearken to us, so sinful, possessed by grief, diseases and many sorrows and come to

our aid with thy holy prayers, which turn the Lord's tender-loving heart to all who cry out to thee:

Rejoice, O fervent intercessor for us before God;

Rejoice, O zealous mediator for us sinners before God.

Rejoice, thou who teachest us to endure the diseases and sorrows with gratitude;

Rejoice, thou who instillest in our hearts the good thoughts in times of confusion.

Rejoice, thou who helpest us with thy prayers to be saved;

Rejoice, thou who dost not leave those who are bodily far from thee but wholeheartedly call to thee.

Rejoice, O Blessed Eldress Matrona, most wondrous wonderworker.

Kontakion 11
Thou, O Honorable Mother Matrona, art hearing the unearthly angelic singing. While still living on earth thou wast found worthy of conversing with the angels of Heaven, invisibly to those around thee. So also teach us, the unworthy, to properly glorify God, honored in the Trinity: the Father and the Son and the Holy Spirit, to Whom the heavenly hosts unceasingly sing with great voices: Alleluia.

Ikos 11

Thy life, O Blessed Eldress Matrona, shineth with the radiant light illumining the darkness of this exceedingly vain world and drawth to itself our souls so that they would be enlightened even if with little measure of the grace of God and would be able to walk in the manner pleasing to God the sorrowful and narrow path of this life, and reach the gates of the Kingdom of God, where thou, O Mother, we believe, hast now entered. Hear the voice of those calling thee:

Rejoice, O light of God, who enlightenest us even after thy death;

Rejoice, O precious pearl, who illuminatest us with the radiance of thy holiness.

Rejoice, thou who makest us strong in Orthodoxy with the light of thy good deeds;

Rejoice, O fragrant flower, who perfumest our souls with the Holy Spirit.

Rejoice, for all thy life was holy and righteous;

Rejoice, for even thy death was precious before God.

Rejoice, O Blessed Eldress Matrona, most wondrous wonderworker.

Kontakion 12

From the swaddling clothes, thou didst abundantly receive the grace of God, O Blessed Mother, and it remained with thee all thy days: thou didst heal the ailments, drovest away the demons, while foretelling the invisible and the distant and instructing all unto salvation. We believe without doubt that after thy death this grace is even greater with thee. For this sake, we fall down and pray: Do not deprive us also, who are still sojourning on earth, of thy help and protection, as thou beseechest the Lord to have mercy and forgive all who zealously send up to Him in our holy temples the triumphant hymn: Alleluia.

Ikos 12

Singing thy wonders, O Mother Matrona, we praise God Who gave thee such a grace, and with the Prophet David we sing a psalm, for praise befits the upright:

Rejoice, for the Lord loveth the righteous;

Rejoice, for the Lord maketh the blind wise.

Rejoice, for the Lord preserveth all who love Him;

Rejoice, for the Lord's good will is about His people.

Rejoice, for the Lord doeth the will of those who fear Him, and He heareth their prayer and saveth them;

Rejoice, for the Venerable Ones will be exalted in glory and rejoice on their beds.

Rejoice, O Blessed Eldress Matrona, most wondrous wonderworker.

Kontakion 13

O Blessed Mother, hear the song of praise that we sing now and our prayer, for thou didst promise that even after thy death thou wouldest hear those who cry to thee; beseech the Saviour, Our Lord Jesus Christ, to grant us forgiveness of our sins, Christian ending to our lives and the good answer at His Dreadful Judgment, so that we together with all who are pardoned by God be found worthy, in the paradisiacal abodes, to glorify the Holy Trinity with the beautiful singing: Alleluia (Thrice).

Ikos 1 and Kontakion 1 are repeated

Prayers to Blessed Eldress Matrona

First Prayer

O Blessed Mother Matrona, hearken unto us and receive us now, the sinful people who pray to thee, for in thy life thou didst become accustomed to receive and hear out all the suffering and the sorrowful, who hastened with faith and hope to thy protection and help, granting all speedy help and miraculous healing. May thy mercy not grow scarce even now towards us, the unworthy, restless in this exceedingly vain world, for we cannot find anywhere consolation and compassion for our sorrowful souls and our ailing bodies. Heal our diseases, deliver us from temptations and torments from the devil who vehemently wageth war against us, help us bear the Cross of our everyday life to the end and patiently endure the hardships of this life, and not to lose the image of God, and to preserve the Orthodox Faith till the end of our days, to have a strong hope and trust in God and unhypocritical love for our neighbors. Help us, after departure from this life, to reach the Heavenly Kingdom together with all those who pleased God, glorifying mercy and goodness of the Heavenly Father, glorified in the Trinity, the Father and the Son and the Holy Spirit, unto the ages of ages. Amen.

Second Prayer

O Blessed Mother Matrona, with thy soul thou standest now before the Throne of God, and restest on earth with thy body, and thou streamest forth diverse miracles by the grace given thee from on high. Look down with thy merciful eyes upon us sinners, who spend our days in sorrows, illnesses and demonic temptations. Comfort us the despairing ones, heal our cruel diseases, which have been allowed by God because of our sins, deliver us from our many misfortunes and evil circumstance. Entreat Our Lord Jesus Christ to forgive us all our transgressions, iniquities and fallings into sin, which we have committed from our youth even unto the present day and hour, so that receiving grace by thy prayers, we may glorify the one God in Trinity, Father, Son and Holy Spirit, now and ever and unto the ages of ages. Amen.

Troparia to Blessed Eldress Matrona

Troparion, tone 2

O faithful, let us praise today, the Blessed Eldress Matrona, made wise by God, a blossom of the land of Tula and all-glorious adornment of the city of Moscow. For not knowing the light of day, she was enlightened by the light of Christ and was enriched by gifts of insight and healing. She was a sojourner and pilgrim on earth, and now in the heavenly chambers she standth and prayth for our souls before the Throne of God.

Troparion, tone 4

A sprout of the land of Tula, an angel-like warrior of the city of Moscow, O Blessed Eldress Matrona! In the bodily blindness thou wast from thy birth to the end of thy days, but thou didst receive from God the spiritual vision abundantly, O one of clairvoyance and prayer. Moreover, thou didst acquire the exceptional gift of healing of diseases. Come to the aid of all those who with faith hasten unto thee and beseeching thee in their spiritual and bodily diseases, O our joy!

Kontakion, tone 7

Thou wast forechosen for the service of Christ from thy mother's womb, O Righteous Matrona, thou didst travel the path of sorrows and grief and didst show forth steadfast faith and piety, thou didst please God. Therefore, honoring thy memory, we pray to thee: help us to abide in the love of God, O Blessed Eldress.

Magnification

We magnify thee, O Holy Righteous Eldress Matrona, and we honor thy holy memory, for thou dost pray for us to Christ Our God.

Refrain

O Holy Blessed Mother Matrona, pray to God for us.

Gospel

(Luke 7:36-50, Beginning 33) At that time, one of the Pharisees desired him that he would eat with him. And he went into the Pharisee's house, and sat down to meat. And, behold, a woman in the city, which was a sinner, when she knew that Jesus sat at meat in the Pharisee's house, brought an alabaster box of ointment, and stood at his feet behind him weeping, and began to wash his feet with tears, and did wipe them with the hairs of her head, and kissed his feet, and anointed them with the ointment. Now when the Pharisee which had bidden him saw it, he spake within himself, saying, This man, if he were a prophet, would have known who and what manner of woman this is that toucheth him: for she is a sinner. And Jesus answering said unto him, Simon, I have somewhat to say unto thee. And he saith, Master, say on. There was a certain creditor which had two debtors: the one owed five hundred pence, and the other fifty. And when they had nothing to pay, he frankly forgave them both. Tell me therefore, which of them will love him most? Simon answered and said, I suppose that he, to whom he forgave most. And he said unto him, Thou hast rightly judged. And he turned to the woman, and said unto Simon, Seest thou this woman? I entered into thine house, thou gavest me no water for my feet: but she hath washed my feet with tears, and wiped them with the hairs of her head. Thou gavest me no kiss: but this woman since the time I came in hath not ceased to kiss my feet. My head with oil thou didst not anoint: but this woman hath anointed my feet with ointment. Wherefore I say unto thee, Her sins, which are many, are forgiven; for she loved much: but to whom little is forgiven, the same loveth little. And he said unto her, Thy sins are forgiven. And they that sat at meat with him began to say within themselves, Who is this that forgiveth sins also? And he said to the woman, Thy faith hath saved thee; go in peace.

"Blessed Saint Matrona, pray to God for us to keep us safe from all evil, invisible and visible."

"Blessed Matrona, hear and receive those
who pray to you."

Books by Ariane Trifunovic Montemuro:

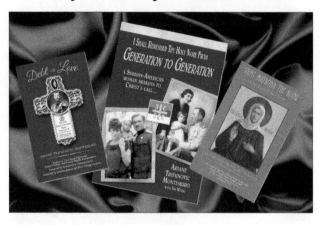

*left to right:
**Debt of Love, I Shall Remember Thy Holy Name From
Generation to Generation,** *and* **Saint Matrona the Blind:
Our Friend in Christ** *are available at*
all major online booksellers.

I was up late last night reading *Debt of Love.* It is truly inspiring and filled with so much grace. I couldn't stop the tears.

— JONATHAN JACKSON
Emmy Award-winning American Actor

Wonderful, Heartwarming & Prayerful. 5 Stars. Ariane says in the beginning [of *Generation to Generation*] that this is a letter to her children, but really it's a letter to all of us Orthodox Christians in America and beyond. It is a testament to our citizenship belonging in Heaven, no matter where we are from or where we have moved to.

— MILICA MINIC
Missionary Administrator
Orthodox Christian Mission Center

ENDNOTES

i

Troparion of Saint Matrona of Moscow and Ikos 1 were provided by Holy Trinity Monastery, Jordanville, NY

ii

The Life of Blessed Matrona of Moscow commemorated April 19/May 2, OrthoChristian. com, page 12. Accessed 2/11/2020.

iii

Ibid.

iv

How to live a Holy Life, Metropolitan Gregory (Postnikov), 1904, translated by Seraphim F. Englehardt, 2005, Published by the Printshop of Saint Job of Pochaev, Holy Trinity Monastery, Jordanville, NY 2005, p. 10.

v

James 5:16, KJV.

vi

The Life of Blessed Matrona of Moscow, OrthoChristian.com, Page 2 of 18 pages, Accessed 2/11/2020.

vii

Ibid, Page 3 of 18 pages.

viii

Blessed Saint Matrona of Moscow, by Sister Ioanna, St. Innocent Monastic Community, Redford Michigan, Page 3 of 3.

ix

Ibid.

x

Ibid.

xi

Blind Saint with Sight: St Matrona of Moscow (1885-1952) American Carpatho-Russian Orthodox Diocese of the U.S.A. Page 2 of 3. Accessed 10/20/2020.

xii

Ibid.

xiii

Blessed Saint Matrona of Moscow, by Sister Ioanna, St. Innocent Monastic Community, Redford Michigan, Page 3 of 3.

xiv

Blind Saint with Sight: St Matrona of Moscow (1885-1952) American Carpatho-Russian Orthodox Diocese of the U.S.A. Page 3 of 3. Accessed 10/20/2020.

xv

Ibid.

xvi

The Life of Blessed Matrona of Moscow
Commemorated April 19/May 2, page 3 of 18,
OrthoChristian.com. Accessed 12/13/2019.

xvii

The life of Blessed Matrona of Moscow, Pravoslavie.
ru, Page 17 of 18. Accessed 12/13/2019.

xviii

Full of Grace and Truth: Saint Matrona of Moscow,
full-of-grace-and-truth.blogspot.com/2009/05/
st-matrona-of-moscow.html. Page 9 of 21. Accessed
3/3/2020.

xix

*Mystagogy, An Orthodox Christian Weblog of the
Mystagogy Resource Center*, May 2, 2009 Saint
Matrona the Blind of Moscow. Pages 3 and 4 of 7.
Accessed 10/20/2020.

xx

Full of Grace and Truth: Saint Matrona of Moscow,
full-of-grace-and-truth.blogspot.com/2009/05/
st-matrona-of-moscow.html Pages 5 and 6 of 21
pages. Accessed 3/3/2020.

xxi

The Life of Blessed Matrona of Moscow,
Commemorated April 19/May 2. http://
Pravoslavie.ru /79033.html, Page 8 of 18. Accessed
4/12/2020.

xxii
"Road to Emmaus," *A Journal of Orthodox Faith and Culture*, Vol. VIII, No. 1 (#28), page 14 of 25.

xxiii
Ibid, page 10 of 25.

xxiv
Ibid, page 14 of 25.

xxv
Ibid, page 18 of 25.

xxvi
"Archbishop Leonty of Chile: Confessor of Heartfelt Orthodoxy," reprinted from the *Orthodox Word*, Vol. 17, No. 4(99) July-August 1981.

xxvii
Miraculous Help from Blessed Matrona of Moscow in Our Day. Pravoslavie.ru/101691.html. Pages 3 and 4 of 10. Accessed 10/20/2020.

xxviii
Ibid, page 1 of 10.

xxix
Ibid, pages 2 and 3 of 10.

xxx
Ibid, page 1 of 10.

xxxi
Ibid, page 2 of 10.

xxxii
Flowers for Matronushka, Leonid Garkotin.
Orthochristian.com/111325.html, pages 1-3.
Accessed 10/20/2020.

xxxiii
Saint Justin Popovich, Orthodox Faith and Life in Christ (Belmont, Mass.: Institute for Byzantine and Modern Greek Studies, 1994), pp. 35-36.

xxxiv
"The Place of Lives of Saints in the Spiritual Life," by Hieromonk Damascene, A Talk delivered at the Annual Assembly of the Serbian Orthodox Dioceses of Western America, Feb. 16/March 1, 2002 Orthodoxinfo.com/general/place_lives.aspx

xxxv
Ibid.

xxxvi
The Akathist to Blessed Eldress Matrona of Moscow was provided by Holy Trinity Monastery, Jordanville, New York